Macmillan Computer Science Series

Consulting Editor: Professor F. H. Sumner, University of Manchester

A. Abdellatif, J. Le Bihan and M. Limame, *Oracle – A User's guide*
Ian O. Angell, *High-resolution Computer Graphics Using C*
Ian O. Angell and Gareth Griffith, *High-resolution Computer Graphics Using FORTRAN 77*
Ian O. Angell and Gareth Griffith, *High-resolution Computer Graphics Using Pascal*
M. Azmoodeh, *Abstract Data Types and Algorithms, second edition*
C. Bamford and P. Curran, *Data Structures, Files and Databases, second edition*
P. Beynon-Davies, *Information Systems Development, second edition*
G.M. Birtwistle, *Discrete Event Modelling on Simula*
Linda E.M. Brackenbury, *Design of VLSI Systems – A Practical Introduction*
Alan Bradley, *Peripherals for Computer Systems*
G.R. Brookes and A.J. Stewart, *Introduction to occam 2 on the Transputer*
P.C. Capon and P.J. Jinks, *Compiler Engineering Using Pascal*
Robert Cole, *Computer Communications, second edition*
E. Davalo and P. Naïm, *Neural Networks*
S.M. Deen, *Principles and Practice of Database Systems*
D. England *et al.*, *A Sun User's Guide, second edition*
Jean Ettinger, *Programming in C++*
J.S. Florentin, *Microprogrammed Systems Design*
A.B. Fontaine and F. Barrand, *80286 and 80386 Microprocessors*
Michel Gauthier, *Ada – A Professional Course*
M.G. Hartley, M. Healey and P.G. Depledge, *Mini and Microcomputer Systems*
J.A. Hewitt and R.J. Frank, *Software Engineering in Modula-2 – An Object-oriented Approach*
M.J. King and J.P. Pardoe, *Program Design Using JSP – A Practical Introduction, second edition*
Bernard Leguy, *Ada – A Programmer's Introduction*
M. Léonard, *Database Design Theory*
David Lightfoot, *Formal Specification Using Z*
A.M. Lister and R.D. Eager, *Fundamentals of Operating Systems, fifth edition*
Elizabeth Lynch, *Understanding SQL*
B. A. E. Meekings, T. P. Kudrycki and M. D. Soren, *A Book on C, third edition*
R. J. Mitchell, *C++ Object-Oriented Programming*
R.J. Mitchell, *Microcomputer Systems Using the STE Bus*
R.J. Mitchell, *Modula-2 Applied*
Y. Nishinuma and R. Espesser, *UNIX – First Contact*
Pham Thu Quang and C. Chartier-Kastler, *MERISE in Practice*

Continued overleaf

Macmillan Computer Science Series (continued)

Ian Pratt, *Artificial Intelligence*
E.J. Redfern, *Introduction to Pascal for Computational Mathematics*
Gordon Reece, *Microcomputer Modelling by Finite Differences*
F. D. Rolland, *Programming with VDM*
L.E. Scales, *Introduction to Non-Linear Optimization*
A.G. Sutcliffe, *Human–Computer Interface Design, second edition*
Colin J. Theaker and Graham R. Brookes, *Concepts of Operating Systems*
M. Thorin, *Real-time Transaction Processing*
M.R. Tolhurst *et al.*, *Open Systems Interconnection*

Non-series
I.O. Angell and D. Tsoubelis, *Advanced Graphics on VGA and XGA Cards using Borland C++*
N. Frude, *A Guide to SPSS/PC+, second edition*
Percy Mett, *Introduction to Computing*
Tony Royce, *COBOL – An Introduction*
Tony Royce, *Structured COBOL – An Introduction*
Tony Royce, *C Programming – An Introduction*

Concepts
of
Operating Systems

Colin J. Theaker

Staffordshire University

and

Graham R. Brookes

Hull University

MACMILLAN

First published 1993 by
MACMILLAN PRESS LTD
Houndmills, Basingstoke, Hampshire RG21 6XS
and London
Companies and representatives
throughout the world

This text is a revised and expanded edition of
A Practical Course on Operating Systems, by the same authors,
first published in 1983

ISBN 0–333–52366–0

A catalogue record for this book is available
from the British Library.

10   9   8   7   6   5   4   3   2
04   03   02   01   00   99   98   97   96

Printed in Hong Kong

Contents

Preface

An operating system is one of the most important pieces of software in any modern computer system, irrespective of its size or application, yet much mystique still surrounds its design. Operating systems themselves seek to be transparent to users, which adds to their perception as a black box. As computer systems increase in complexity, particularly at the microprocessor level, more complexity appears in the system software. It is easy to forget that the operating system is not an end in itself; it is there solely to provide efficient support for other activities. With this in mind, the primary objective of this book is to provide a greater practical understanding of the concepts of the design and implementation of operating systems, the problems they address and the constraints imposed on them.

This book has been produced as an update on an earlier text *A Practical Course on Operating Systems* by the same authors. The subject of operating systems has advanced substantially since the earlier text, as the ideas of what operating systems should do are constantly being modified by changing user expectations and requirements, and through the increased potential of the system hardware due to technological developments. Whilst this book focuses on the basic concepts of operating systems, many of which are long standing, it has been necessary to make substantial revision of the earlier material in producing this book. The ordering of much of the material has been changed, some aspects such as treatment of traditional Job Control Languages have been deleted, and new topics such as Networking have been introduced.

The contents of this book are derived from a number of courses of lectures given to undergraduate students of computer science. In its entirety, it provides suitable material for a full course on operating systems for students who have a basic grounding in computer science or who have some practical experience of computing. Less detailed courses may be derived by choosing a sub-section of chapters. For example, the first two chapters provide an overview of the structure of an operating system, and can therefore be used as material for a lower level course that seeks to provide a general introduction to the nature and role of operating systems. By focusing on concepts rather than the current flavour of any particular operating system, the text is also of interest to software engineers involved in the development of embedded systems, as the problems faced at the hardware interface are identical, albeit in different guises.

This book differs significantly from other operating systems texts in the way in which the material is presented. The intention has been to provide a sound understanding of the underlying concepts, particularly from the point of view of the problems that the operating system is trying to solve. A typical subject will therefore be considered initially by examining the problem area and then introducing possible solutions. These may reflect chronological developments, changes in technology or levels of sophistication within the systems.

Although this approach may appear as being 'bottom-up', the authors feel that it has strength in providing an appreciation of basic concepts and rationale. It provides an understanding of the constraints, interfaces and problems faced by operating system software, without losing sight of the end objectives. In contrast, the more traditional way of examining the subject is from the 'outside looking in', where one might see a complete operating system, with all its sophistication and vagaries. Although good for examining particular systems, to stand back and admire the handiwork of others might not provide a sound understanding of the rationale.

The first two chapters of this book provide essential background on which further detailed consideration of topics follow. Chapter 1 identifies why operating systems are necessary, provides a brief historical view of their developments and surveys major types of operating system from the point of view of their application. Chapter 2 introduces basic concepts relating to the structure of operating systems. The notion of a process is described, together with the use of interrupts and multiprogramming. An outline of a simple operating system design is developed, initially using a simple spooling system as the vehicle, and subsequently extending the ideas to the realisation of a time sharing system. This system provides the platform on which other more advanced topics are developed within the text. Further coverage of this system design is also provided in the appendix.

Chapter 3 provides an examination of input/output management techniques. Although not fundamental to the overall structure and operation of a system, it picks up on topics introduced in chapter 2 to complete the coverage of this material. This is followed in chapter 4 by an examination of scheduling principles and the algorithms associated with scheduling. In particular, time slicing is considered in more depth, including its effect on the responsiveness of the system.

A comprehensive treatment of memory management strategies follows in chapters 5 and 6. Starting from the practicalities of supporting the simple system discussed in chapter 2, the notions of protection and virtual memory are introduced, using a simple base-limit register scheme for address translation. Segmentation is described as a means of resolving issues of program locality and sharing, and paging is presented as a solution to fragmentation problems. The chapters conclude with a consideration of memory management algorithms and their associated performance.

Chapter 7 considers the issues that relate to the design of file management systems. The chapter also examines the design of the UNIX file system, being one of the more distinguishing features of that particular operating system.

The chapters so far have largely been concerned with the major functional components or processes within an operating system. Chapters 8 to 12 relate to techniques that are applicable to many different processes, and indeed to supporting the overall process structure. Chapter 8 examines the problems of resource management from the point of view of allocation of resources, competition for their control and the potential for deadlocks. This is followed by a formal review of protection systems, identifying where and how they might be implemented within an operating system.

The problems of concurrency are then examined, and approaches for achieving co-operation and synchronisation of processes are described. Chapter 10 identifies the low level issues that affect co-operating processes. As a primitive solution, the semaphore mechanism is presented, including examples of its use and how it might be implemented. Chapters 11 and 12 discuss higher level approaches to the problem. Firstly language-based approaches are discussed. The functions provided are related to those of the more primitive semaphore mechanism, without addressing the wider issues of their implementation for distributed computing. Other language-based facilities to support the development of system software, such as process management, i/o handling, etc. are also discussed briefly. Message-based approaches are then examined, including the practical considerations that affect their application. The use of messages in a distributed context are also considered, particularly in the implementation of a remote procedure calling mechanism.

The theme of distributed processing is carried further in chapter 13, where issues of networking and interworking are considered. Although networking is playing a more significant role in the use of computers generally, it can be viewed as an enabling technology to support the more fundamental aspects of operating systems. The topic is therefore considered in this light, and readers wishing a more comprehensive coverage of networking issues are referred to specialist texts on the subject.

The final chapter addresses issues relating to the overall performance of the system. As with the engineering of any product, it is important to be able to quantify the effectiveness of any design and implementation. This is not always easy to achieve in the case of an operating system owing to its primary role in supporting other applications. Chapter 14 surveys techniques for the monitoring and evaluation of system performance and reviews the use of such information.

An appendix provides a more detailed specification of a simple operating system. It provides simple time sharing facilities, similar to the system introduced in chapter 2, and employs input/output, scheduling, memory and file management techniques, as discussed in chapters 3-7. The system design has deliberately been kept simple for illustrative purposes, and exercises are provided to allow readers to develop more sophisticated implementations.

Throughout the book, specific cases and examples of systems are considered to illustrate general points made in the text. At the end of chapters, there are references to which readers can find more detailed information on specific topics.

Colin J Theaker

Graham R Brookes

1   Overview

We shall begin our consideration of operating systems by posing a number of questions for discussion.

1.1 What is an operating system?

An operating system is the most basic program within a computer system. It is there to provide a service and to help users to run their applications; as such, it is a 'means to an end'.

In simple terms, an operating system is just like any other program, although it differs from most other programs in a few important ways. For example, it might be able to perform certain operations that are not available to normal user programs, such as having direct control of peripherals and access to special machine registers. It is regarded as *privileged* in that respect. Once started, the operating system must keep running until the computer system is shut down. It is therefore expected to be both reliable and efficient, more so than other programs.

These criteria, among others, may be used to distinguish between an operating system and other *system software*, such as compilers, editors etc.

1.2 Why are operating systems needed?

This is a particularly relevant question, as operating systems are often viewed as a nuisance, getting in the way of users when they want to do something. It is worth stating the basic objectives that an operating system is seeking to attain:

(1) to manage the resources of the computer system according to predefined 'fair', efficient and secure strategies, and

(2) to provide a more convenient interface with the hardware, relieving the applications software of the low level control functions.

Operating systems attempt to satisfy both of these objectives although, in practice, these requirements are not mutually exclusive and a compromise in design has to be made. This is also the reason why they are often viewed as

1

obstructive, as the functionality provided for users and applications must be balanced by the overall objectives of managing the resources according to the policy defined for the system.

The following list illustrates the sort of services that an operating system might provide to help the user run a program. They provide an abstraction of the real machine in a form where the functionality is more convenient to use. They are therefore analogous to the existence of assemblers and compilers, that allow a user to write a program without needing to know the binary format of machine instructions.

Convenient input/output operations

The details of how a particular peripheral has to be controlled in order to read or print a character is hidden by device driving software.

Fault monitoring

When errors in a program are detected, the operating system intervenes to record the program state and to print suitable monitoring information to help the user find the source of the fault. Various levels of monitoring information may be printed, some by the operating system, some by the compiler or run-time support system of the programming language.

File systems

The operating system maintains the directories and is responsible for the security of a user's files. Centralised control is necessary in order to allow several users to share the same hardware while maintaining a secure file system where the files of each user are protected from invalid access.

1.3 Must there always be an operating system?

In theory, the answer could be 'No'. Computers which are used for very specific purposes, where the application does not change, and there is no requirement to provide the development facilities normally associated with general purpose systems, might not have a separate recognisable operating system. For example, a dedicated system for an embedded application, such as providing control functions within an industrial plant, would run software specifically developed for that application.

The main distinction between general purpose and dedicated systems is that the workload of general purpose systems may vary quite significantly and dynamically, so flexibility is paramount. A wide range of facilities would be provided as the precise requirements of each user are unknown and each user might want different functionality. Dedicated systems are intended for a specific application, and as the characteristics of the application would normally be well defined and understood, the functionality and performance requirements of the operating system can be optimised for that application.

Dedicated systems may arise in a number of different application areas. For example, specific nodes within a computer network may have a dedicated role, such as providing a transaction processing capability or acting as a database/file server for other computers. Such a system is likely to be a subset of a normal general purpose system. A more widespread example is in embedded applications, where a processor is performing specific control functions, such as within domestic appliances or within engine-management systems of automobiles.

The most significant drive for dedicated systems arises from applications with real-time constraints, as the flexibility inherent in general purpose systems inevitably incurs overheads which affect the performance and responsiveness of the system. Size may also be an important consideration, particularly in providing the necessary functionality in an embedded system where cost constraints are critical.

Nevertheless, there is no escaping the fact that certain basic functions have to be provided within the software, for example, the control of 'peripherals' via an input/output interface. Thus although the operating system functionality has been totally subsumed within the application, in effect, eliminating the operating system *per se*, much of the normal operating system functionality is still present, albeit through a more fuzzy interface. Production of such bespoke systems often employs the use of operating system sub-components which may be specifically configured within the real-time application software.

1.4 Where does an operating system 'live'?

On some small systems, the software exists as code in Read Only Memory (ROM), which ensures that it is always accessible to user programs and cannot be corrupted by the user. However, on most systems, the operating system will exist as files on the disk. A bootstrap program, usually in ROM, loads the operating system from disk into the memory of the computer when the machine is started or reset. Once loaded, some portions of it remain permanently in memory while the computer is running user jobs. It therefore shares the memory with the jobs that it is running. Because an operating system may be very large, other portions of the system are swapped in and out of memory when the facilities are required by the users.

1.5 How do operating systems differ from one another?

Computer-based applications are many and varied, so to provide efficient usage of the system resources and appropriate facilities for the applications, the detailed requirements of the operating system software are correspondingly diverse. The software is also inherently machine dependent so, as a consequence, many different operating systems exist, varying both in functionality and in the required hardware base. Operating systems may be classified in many different ways, including:

> general purpose / dedicated
> single user / multi-access
> uni-programming / multiprogramming (multi-tasking)
> batch / interactive
> networked / distributed / multiprocessing

These terms will be explained further throughout the book. The classifications are not mutually exclusive but reflect different perspectives of a system in terms of its application, capability or organisation.

In this book we shall seek to illustrate the principles behind a range of operating systems, rather than providing a detailed consideration of any specific system, and examples will be given of a number of different system designs.

1.6 How large and complex is the operating system software?

The size and complexity will depend on a number of factors, most notably the characteristics of the computer system, the facilities it has to provide and the nature of the applications it has to support. For example, the operating system for a single user microprocessor can be relatively simple in comparison with that for a large multi-user mainframe computer. However, most of the functions that a system has to support are relatively simple. The software is therefore developed as many small components, rather than as a single large program. An important concept in any practical operating system design is how these components are organised and managed.

Partitioning the operating system into its main functional components provides one form of structuring, but an approach also used is to regard the operating system as a layered object. At the centre is a nucleus of basic facilities, to which additional layers are added as required to provide more sophisticated facilities, in effect adding levels of abstraction. This structure is often considered analogous to the rings of an onion. As an example, consider the following; input/output operations within a program may be provided by record management software within the operating system. This would be concerned primarily with the internal organisation of the data within a file, and would use primitives of a catalogue manager whenever files needed to be opened or closed. The catalogue manager would be responsible for the organisation and management of the directories and the files as a whole. This, in turn, may use the functions of a disk manager for allocating space and performing transfers.

Some operating systems, such as VME/B for the ICL 2900 (Keedy, 1976; Huxtable and Pinkerton, 1977) and UNIX (Ritchie and Thompson, 1974), exhibit this neatly layered structure. Some machines even provide protection systems in the hardware to support such a layered organisation, thus ensuring that even the operating system code has a privilege commensurate with its role.

Rather than starting with such a potentially complex system and decomposing it to identify the important components of the operating system, the approach we intend to take in this book is to concentrate on the concepts behind operating system design. We shall consider the problems that the system is attempting to solve, possible solutions and their limitations, and what improvements and enhancements would be required to provide a powerful and sophisticated system. We thus intend to build up the design of the operating system components in an evolutionary manner, in many respects, reflecting the historical development that has led to the present structure of modern operating systems.

1.7 Historical development

The operating systems of the 1950s, often referred to as the first generation, were designed to improve the overall usage of the computer by reducing the operator/user overheads between jobs. They were characterised by the introduction of *batch processing*, whereby jobs were gathered into batches so that the operator did not need to intervene between the running of individual jobs. Once a given job was running, it had complete control of the machine until either it finished or terminated abnormally, at which point control was passed back to the operating system.

The running of programs during this period was often inconvenient and not particularly 'user friendly'. Jobs were typically submitted on cards to the computer room, and were read by the computer and stored on magnetic tape or disk. Simultaneously the computer would also be running jobs submitted earlier. This technique is known as *spooling* (Simultaneous Peripheral Operation On Line), and was used both for input and output. Whenever the system completed a job, it would fetch a new one from the disk. Early systems of this type were well suited to large scientific calculations and big commercial data processing applications.

The operating systems of the early 1960s, the second generation, were characterised by the development of *multiprogramming*. In multiprogramming systems, several user programs are in main store at any one time and the processor switches between the jobs, running each in turn. The relevance of this became more significant when linked with changes in the user interface to the computer system. By providing access to the system via a terminal, an *interactive* or conversational mode of use results whereby the computer services requests typed by the user as soon as it can. By having multiple terminals connected, the systems have a *multi-access* capability, allowing many users to access the computer simultaneously.

Such potential to respond to external interactions was extended in the emergence of real-time systems in which computers may be used to control industrial processes. In such systems, the interactions are with other forms of input/output devices, rather than users typing on terminals, and a response from the system has to be guaranteed within a specified minimum acceptable response time.

Provision of a multi-access capability imposes additional requirements, such as the scheduling of the workload to ensure that the computer appears responsive to all the users at their terminals. Other areas of importance are in security (both in permitting access to the machine and also in allowing access to files), and in terms of support for the operational management of the system (for example, in maintaining the communications system with the terminals and in backing up or archiving files).

The operating systems from the mid 1960s to the end of the 1970s, the third generation, were designed to be powerful general purpose systems, supporting simultaneously batch, interactive and real-time processing. By recognising the different types of workload, in principle the operating system can maintain a balance between good system efficiency and responsiveness to interactions. On some systems, the distinction was acknowledged even further by using multiple processors to run the different types of workload, where a front-end processor handles the interactive work and a back-end processor is optimised for batch processing.

The disadvantage with such systems is that they were large, expensive to produce and maintain, and their inherent complexity produced an effective additional software layer between the user and the hardware. Complex job control languages were developed to allow a user to interface with the system. Typical of this generation were the systems produced by IBM for their 360 range of machines.

Such large and unwieldy systems often gave poor response, particularly for users with small jobs and for people engaged in debugging programs, and this extended the need to provide better time-sharing systems for interactive use. The desire to provide a computer capable of supporting many simultaneous time-sharing users led to the production of MULTICS (MULTiplexed Information and Computing Service) (Corbato and Vyssotsky, 1965), whose development played a significant role in the design of future generations of operating systems.

It was during this third generation that there was a large growth in the production of minicomputers, which had started with the DEC PDP-1 in 1961. Several machines followed from DEC, leading to the range of PDP-11s. It was in producing a single-user version of MULTICS for the PDP-7 that UNICS (UNiplexed Information and Computing Service) came into existence. This has since been respelt (and redeveloped) to give the UNIX system (Ritchie and Thompson, 1974) which is so popular today.

With the advances in the development of Large Scale Integrated (LSI) circuits and the inception of microprocessors, the 1980s or fourth generation saw the emergence of microcomputers or personal computers. These formed a logical progression from the minicomputer of the PDP-11 class, and were characterised by a user friendly system, lacking in complexity and requiring little knowledge of the system itself. There was no need for the complications of the powerful job control languages which had been so much a feature of the early mainframe computers. Although many more manufacturers were now producing computer systems, largely based on a small number of different microprocessors, the trend has been towards standardising on operating systems, with UNIX and MS-DOS dominant in this area.

The early development of microcomputers was for stand-alone, single-user systems. Such systems had very simple operating system requirements as the resource management problems inherent in mainframe computer systems, such as the security and integrity of the file store, were often delegated to the user. Such microcomputer systems are now increasing in sophistication as the processor power and memory capacity increase. For example, personal computer systems now provide a multiprogramming capability, which allows background tasks to execute in parallel with the main interactive activity. Although such systems have similar process support and scheduling requirements to those of the larger multi-access mainframe systems, they are still considerably more simple by virtue of being single user without the same operational or integrity constraints.

The technological developments that led to the production of microprocessors have resulted in the emergence of a number of other system structures, which allow multiple processors to be interconnected to provide more powerful facilities. The most common of these are networked systems.

In this case, each computer system is capable of operating as an independent entity, but can also call upon services at other machines by sending messages across the network. The operating system provides the basic mechanism for transporting these messages. The range of networked services or *interworking* functions is very open-ended, and systems typically include facilities such as file transfer, electronic mail and remote log-in capabilities.

A further class of operating system is the distributed system. This also involves multiple processors, and in many respects the interconnection technology may be similar to the networked systems outlined. However, the logical binding between the machines is much tighter, as collectively the machines behave as a single system with the functions of the operating system distributed between the various nodes. Some nodes may have very specific functions, for example, in a cluster of workstations, one may be equipped with disk storage and acts as the file server and backing store for the others. In general, the system topology is invisible to the users, who are unaware of which networked processors are running their programs or where their files are located. This information is managed by the operating system.

Distributed systems may be considerably more complex than single processor operating systems, and are not merely extensions of them. Since programs may execute on one of several processors, the scheduling algorithms are more complex so as to try to optimise the amount of parallelism. In a single processor system, the operating system has complete knowledge of the entire system state, whereas this is not the case in a distributed system because of the effects of communication delays. Also in the case of distributed systems, the need for fault tolerance means that there is a desire that at least part of the system will continue to function even if another part is broken.

Similar operating system characteristics may be seen in a multiprocessor configuration. This is normally viewed as a single, very high performance machine, where the coupling between the processors is very tight. The communications medium is typically shared memory, although some machines also use high performance direct point-to-point links for communication. Such systems achieve a higher processing capability by distributing the workload, in the form of multiple processes, between the available processors. The distribution may be static, for example assigning predefined tasks to specific processors at compile/program build time. It may also be dynamic, where the intention is to balance the loading of the various processors by allowing tasks to be executed by any available processor. Although dynamic distribution theoretically may achieve higher overall throughput by improving the processor utilisation, it may also incur overheads due to the movement of programs and data between processors, thus offsetting any performance gains.

Technological developments have also led to significant changes in the ways in which we interact with the computer. For example, terminal displays now support a wide range of graphic operations, with high resolution and colour. The use of keyboards as a means of accessing a computer system has been extended by the use of pointing and picking devices, such as mice, to select and manipulate icons on the screen, and WIMP interfaces (Windows, Icons, Mice, Pull-down menus) are very common. This type of interface has resulted in the rather archaic job control languages characteristic of mainframe computers becoming practically obsolete for many computer users.

One of the most striking developments has been that of window management systems. With window management, it is possible to have two different objectives dependent on whether the requirement is to have a single window per session or many windows. In the first case, the window management system provides a means whereby the user can switch attention between multiple independent tasks. In the latter case, support is provided for complex operations which wish to use multiple display windows to support a complex dialogue. This is illustrated by systems such as Smalltalk-80, and Interlisp-D. X-windows, NEWS (Network Extensible Window System) and MS-Windows are typical of current window management systems.

Clearly the scope of operating systems is very great, and many different systems exist with varied objectives and characteristics. The significant features which characterise any particular system arise from the functions provided and the ways in which they are implemented. Operating systems would typically include components to perform the following:

Input/Output
Process Management and Scheduling
Memory Management
File Systems
Resource Management
Interprocess Communication
Networking Facilities

As the structure of operating systems is very open-ended, specific systems may include other areas of functionality, or similarly omit some entirely. This list therefore represents a cross-section of the facilities found in most general purpose systems. Further chapters within this book will cover the principles behind the design of these components, with illustrations from existing systems.

Before covering these topics in detail, some basic concepts relating to the design of operating systems as a whole are covered, including topics relating to the behaviour and structuring of an operating system.

1.8 References and bibliography

D.W.Barron (1974). 'Job Control Languages and Job Control Programs', *Computer Journal*, Vol 17, pp. 282-86.

F.J. Corbato and V.A. Vyssotsky (1965). 'Introduction and Overview of the MULTICS System', *Proc. AFIPS Fall Joint Computer Conference*, pp. 185-96.

P.J. Denning (1982). 'Are Operating Systems Obsolete', *Communications of the ACM*, Vol 25, pp. 225-27.

D.H.R. Huxtable and J.M.M. Pinkerton (1977). 'The Hardware/Software Interface of the ICL2900 Range of Computers', *Computer Journal*, Vol. 20, pp. 290-5.

J.L. Keedy (1976). 'The Management and Technological Approach to the design of System B', *Proc. 7th Australian Computer Conf.*, Perth, pp. 997-1013.

Microsoft Corporation (1986). *Microsoft MS-DOS User's Reference*, Microsoft Press, Redmond, Oregon.

Microsoft Corporation (1986). *Microsoft MS-DOS Programmer's Reference*, Microsoft Press, Redmond, Oregon.

D.M. Ritchie and K. Thompson (1974). 'The UNIX Time-sharing System', *Communications of the ACM*, Vol. 17, pp. 365-75.

N. Weizer (1981). 'A History of Operating Systems', *Datamation*, Vol. 1, pp. 119-26.

2   Basic Concepts

The overriding objective of any operating system has always been to manage the resources under its control in the most effective way possible. In early computer systems, this was essential as the computer itself was a valuable resource in very short supply. Through technological developments, processing power is now a much more expendable commodity, although many applications still demand good performance and a high efficiency from the system.

The availability of processing power has significantly changed the way in which we use computer systems, but the efficient use of resources is still paramount. The main difference is how we classify 'resources'. Even activities which are particularly extravagant in terms of the memory and processor power that they consume, such as sophisticated window management systems and user interfaces, are intended to support the productivity of users and as such are a system concern.

This chapter examines the basic concepts which apply to most operating systems. They will usually be illustrated with examples of particular historical significance, largely because the early systems were simple to comprehend and were very specific in the problems that they were addressing. Most of these problems were concerned with resourcing issues. Although overall system designs have progressed significantly with successive generations of computers and of operating systems, many of the same basic concepts are still applicable. Indeed, many popular current systems still exhibit their long standing 'roots'.

2.1 Processes

The term *process* is open to very wide interpretation. It could be used to describe the 'process' that the user is trying to perform, which may involve running many programs concurrently. It might also describe the environment for executing a single program or sequence of code. It is often used interchangeably with the term *task*, with different nomenclature being favoured by different system designers.

The most common interpretation, and the one that will be used within this book, is that a process is 'a program in execution'. In this sense, a process

11

consists of the executable program code, the program's data (and stack), registers for controlling the execution, such as the program counter and stack pointer, and all other information which must be available to run the program. These items are often referred to as the *context* of the process.

A process frequently equates to a unit of work, for example, a job submitted to perform a data processing task as a background activity, or an interactive terminal session involving software development. Multiple processes may cooperate to perform a more complex task on behalf of a user, and this also provides a way of exploiting parallelism in the hardware of the computer system.

During its lifetime, a process may go through a series of discrete states, such as *ready, running* and *blocked.* These indicate whether the program is able to execute but is waiting to be scheduled, whether it has actually been scheduled and is the current program running within the processor, or whether it is halted waiting for some other activity to take place.

2.2 Principles of multiprogramming

Multiprogramming is principally concerned with supporting a number of processes concurrently within the computer, so that, at appropriate times, the CPU can switch from running one process. The process change may be made in order to make optimal use of the resources available, but it may also be constrained by other requirements, such as providing acceptable response times to interactive users on terminals.

An initial incentive for multiprogramming arose because of the large disparity in speed between the input/output (I/O) devices and the CPU on early computer systems. On such systems, programs had **direct control** of the I/O devices. If a program was particularly intensive in terms of input/output activity, it was designated as *input/output-limited*, and the CPU would be idle for most of the time while running the program. Conversely, programs which initiated very few input/output transfers in relation to the processing performed were designated as *CPU-limited*. In general, computer systems must be able to run a variety of jobs and the aim must be to achieve good utilisation of **all** the system's resources under the various conditions. This was particularly important on the early computers, as they were an extremely scarce resource in their own right.

It is possible to postulate a simple arrangement, intending to utilise all resources as much as possible, by multiprogramming a CPU-limited and an input/output-limited job, keeping both in the store together. The input/output-limited job would then be run until it had to wait for a transfer to be completed.

At that point, the CPU-limited job would be scheduled to use up the spare processing capacity. When the peripheral transfer had been completed, a switch back to the input/output-limited job would be made. This processing sequence is illustrated in figure 2.1.

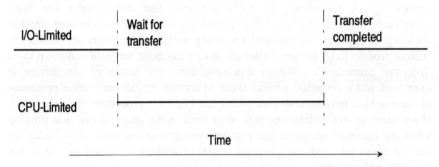

Figure 2.1   Process sequence for simple multiprogramming

The concept of multiprogramming a series of jobs is straightforward; however it is not always possible to have prior knowledge of whether a job is CPU-limited or input/output-limited. Also a job may well change between these two states during its execution; for example, a scientific program which is normally CPU-limited while performing calculations may be input/output-limited when reading its data or printing its results.

The technique of multiprogramming in this way suffers from one major problem, which is that CPU-limited jobs will inevitably need to perform some input/output operations during the course of running. Clearly, when peripherals are controlled directly by each program, the same set of peripherals cannot be used directly by more than one job in the machine as the input and output of the jobs would be unacceptably interleaved. Extra peripherals would therefore be needed for this scheme to work effectively. The alternative strategy which is normally adopted is to delegate control of peripherals to separate device driving processes, which manage the input/output activities on behalf of all users.

2.3 The use of interrupts

In a system that is multiprogramming a number of jobs, the most difficult problem in controlling the peripherals is to determine when a peripheral transfer has been completed. The simplest technique is periodically to examine the control registers associated with a device, but this can be very time-consuming and therefore extremely wasteful, since this time could be used for other more useful operations.

The *interrupt* mechanism is designed to overcome this problem. With this scheme, all peripherals have a special control signal into the CPU. When a device finishes a transfer, such as when an input device has a character available or an output device has printed a character, the peripheral raises this control signal, so telling the CPU hardware that the transfer has been completed. The action of the CPU in servicing this interrupt is to stop obeying the current sequence of instructions, dump sufficient registers to enable the current process to be restarted after the device has been serviced and jump to an 'interrupt procedure'. Within this procedure, the status of the device is examined and appropriate actions taken to service the device. Other processes in the machine may be activated within the interrupt procedure and scheduled. If we return from this interrupt procedure back to the program that was running when the interrupt occurred, the registers dumped at the time of the interrupt can be reloaded, and the program resumed oblivious of the fact that the interrupt had occurred.

An interrupt mechanism is essential if effective multiprogramming of processes is to be achieved. Thus, a process controlling the peripherals will halt while the device is in transfer, and the occurrence of an interrupt is the signal to switch back to it from the currently running process when the transfer has been completed.

2.4 Simple I/O buffering

As mentioned earlier, programs do not perform input, output and processing at such orderly rates that they can keep the CPU and peripherals busy at all times. For example, there may be long periods when the program is computing without performing input/output operations, and yet it would be better to keep the peripherals busy all the time, even through these periods. Basically, a steady flow of characters to and from the peripherals is desirable, even though the program might be consuming the input characters at a very uneven rate and producing the output characters equally irregularly.

The solution, in computing terms, is to use a reservoir or buffer to smooth out the discrepancies between supply and demand. Typically, a complete line of input might be accumulated in the store before it is actually needed. When the program requires the line, it can process it at the speed of the memory rather than the peripheral speed. Similarly, a complete line of output may be buffered in memory by a user program, subsequently to be printed at the speed of the output device.

2.5 Spooling

The performance of a computer system deteriorates significantly when user programs are expected to drive the input and output peripherals directly. This deterioration is, of course, dependent on the extent to which a program is performing input/output operations, but a program that spends most of its time waiting for the completion of peripheral transfers will obviously be using the CPU usefully for very little of the time. In early systems, the CPU was the most expensive commodity and so attempts at improving the CPU efficiency were the main stimulus behind the development of operating systems. To some extent, therefore, the early historical development of operating systems reflects the techniques used to improve the performance.

The disparity in speed between the early CPUs and the conventional peripherals, such as card readers and lineprinters, was the major reason for poor performance, particularly for input/output-limited jobs. The solution initially adopted was to reduce this discrepancy by using only fast peripherals on the main CPU. This technique is epitomised by the IBM systems in the early 1960s which used magnetic tapes as the input and output media on the main CPU, as illustrated in figure 2.2.

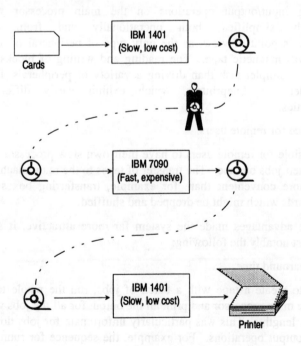

Figure 2.2   Offline spooling system

In offline spooling systems, jobs and their associated data were loaded on to tape using slow, comparatively inexpensive processors. When a batch of jobs had been formed on the tape, the tape was transferred to the main CPU where the jobs and data were read and processed at a relatively fast speed. In a similar way, output from the jobs was written to tape on the main CPU and this was later transferred to the slower processor for printing.

This system had a number of advantages over its simple predecessors where users were responsible for running their own jobs one-at-a-time, namely:

(1) Improved efficiency.

The main processor had a high input/output rate because of the speed of the magnetic tapes. The performance was therefore improved, even for input/output-limited jobs. The slow processors dedicated to servicing the batch peripherals were more closely matched to the speed of the devices and so their efficiency was quite reasonable. The low cost of these processors also made any inefficiency more tolerable.

(2) Simplified operating procedures.

Performing input/output operations on the main processor was considerably simplified, both operationally and from the programmer's point of view, as the only type of peripheral on this machine was magnetic tape. The reading and writing of blocks to tape is a far simpler task than driving a variety of peripherals, like card readers or lineprinters, which exhibit vastly differing characteristics.

(3) Convenience for remote users.

It was possible for remote users to have their own slow processor for spooling their jobs on tape. The transfer of tapes to the main machine was far more convenient than, for example, transferring boxes of punched cards which might be dropped and shuffled.

Although these advantages made the system far more attractive, it still had drawbacks, most notably the following:

(1) Long turnaround time.

The time to create a tape with a batch of jobs, run the whole tape through the main processor and print all the output for all the jobs was often quite lengthy. This was particularly unfortunate for jobs doing few input/output operations. For example, the sequence for running jobs might be

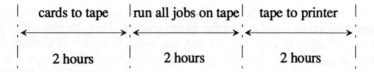

cards to tape	run all jobs on tape	tape to printer
2 hours	2 hours	2 hours

(2) No priority or online access.

The only way of achieving priority access was to take a magnetic tape containing the priority job to the main processor and run it as soon as the processor became free. Even then it might be several hours before the jobs currently being read from tape were fully processed.

(3) Additional hardware required.

In addition to the extra processors for driving the peripherals, there was also quite a lot of extra expense for the magnetic tape drives.

For these reasons, offline spooling as the primary form of input/output was soon superseded, although it remained in use for many years in data preparation for commercial applications, where separate 'key to tape' or 'key to disk' systems were used to verify data and transfer it on to fast media for subsequent input to larger transaction-processing systems.

The major problems of offline spooling are, to some extent, solved by the online spooling system illustrated in figure 2.3.

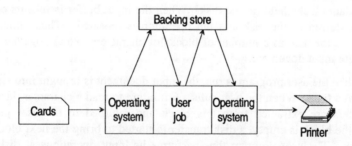

Figure 2.3   Simple online spooling system

In this system, only a single processor is used and a rudimentary spooling operating system co-exists in the processor with a user job. The operating system is multiprogrammed with the user job and transfers data between the slow input/output devices and the backing store (disk or magnetic tape in the early systems). The user job performs its input/output operations to and from the backing store and thus exhibits the same characteristics as in the offline spooling system, where the input/output transfers operate at a fast rate.

To some extent, this situation is analogous to the simple multi-programming case considered earlier in this chapter. Here the operating system is the input/output-limited process and the user job is the CPU-limited one. Unlike the simple case, however, the user job never needs to drive the slow devices directly as all its input/output operations are on documents held on the disk. The timing sequence for this simple multiprogramming case is shown in figure 2.4.

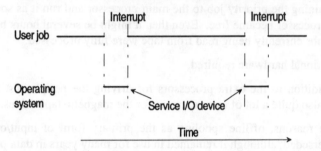

Figure 2.4   Multiprogramming of the operating system with a user job

The passage of a job through this simple spooling system begins with inputting details of the job. The operating system puts the characters which have been read into a buffer in main memory. As disk drives are unable to transfer individual characters, the size of this buffer must correspond to the size of the data blocks held on the disk. When the input buffer is full, its contents are transferred to the disk and the operation is repeated. Thus, input might appear on the disk as a number of blocks of characters, which together form a complete input document.

When the user program is run, the input document is brought into store one block at a time. When the user calls a procedure to read a character, individual characters are extracted from this block and returned to the user program. When the block is empty, a disk transfer is started to bring the next block from the disk. The user program thus performs its input operations at disk speed rather than at the speed of the input device.

A similar sequence operates (in reverse) to form output documents on the disk. These are subsequently brought back into memory by the operating system and printed on the lineprinter. This is illustrated in figure 2.5.

Apart from the actual mechanisms for inputting a job to the system, a very similar scenario exists for many current multiprogramming systems, where large jobs are submitted for running as background processes, not associated with any interactive terminal, and with all their input and output coming from the disk through files.

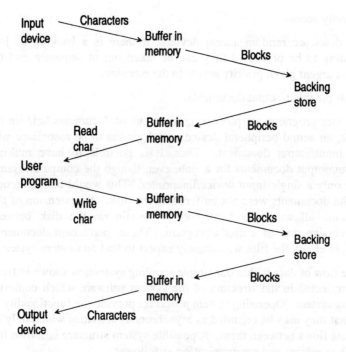

Figure 2.5   Passage of a job through a simple spooling system

As with the offline spooling system, this system has many advantages over the simple example where peripherals are controlled directly by user programs:

(1) Efficient CPU usage.

As with the offline spooling system, input/output operations within the user programs are performed using a fast device (the disk) and thus they run efficiently. The operating system drives the slow peripherals using interrupts, and so this is also efficient in terms of CPU usage.

(2) Efficient peripheral usage.

Building up queues of input and output documents on the disk has a smoothing effect, so that input/output operations can be performed for input/output-limited jobs while running the CPU-limited user jobs.

(3) Fast turnaround.

In contrast with offline spooling, it is not essential to wait for complete input tapes or output tapes to be formed before jobs are run or the output printed.

(4) Priority access.

As disks are random access devices, if there is a backlog of jobs waiting to be processed they can be taken out of sequence and the most urgent given priority access to the machine.

(5) Multiple input/output documents.

As user programs are processing input/output documents held on the disk, an actual peripheral device no longer has to be associated with an input/output document. Thus, it is possible to have multiple input/output documents for a job, even though the computer system has only a single input device/lineprinter. This would be impractical if the documents were not buffered on the disk. An extension of this scheme allows some documents to remain on the disk between successive runs of a user's program. These 'permanent documents' are, in effect, the files we naturally expect to find on modern systems.

The flow of data within our simple spooling system, as shown in figure 2.5, is also reflected in the structure of the system software which comprises our operating system. Operating system *processes* provide the functionality in such a way that they may be regarded as asynchronous activities which only interact when data flows between them. A possible system structure is shown in figure 2.6, with processes and communication as follows:

1 Disk Manager

The Disk Manager coordinates access to the disk, reading and writing input/output blocks on behalf of the Input System and Output System, and the Job Processor running the user program. It is also responsible for managing the free space on the disk, allocating blocks when requested and recovering free space when documents are no longer required. The software would include an interrupt procedure for driving the disk, and interface procedures to be called by the rest of the system to request transfers and manage the free space.

2 Input System

This is synchronised to the operation of the input device, and involves an interrupt procedure which is invoked whenever characters have been read. The characters are packed into a simple buffer in memory, and when the block sized buffer is full, the Disk Manager is requested to initiate a transfer. At the end of an input document, information about the document (such as its location on the disk, size, priority, job name or user name) are passed to the Job Scheduler.

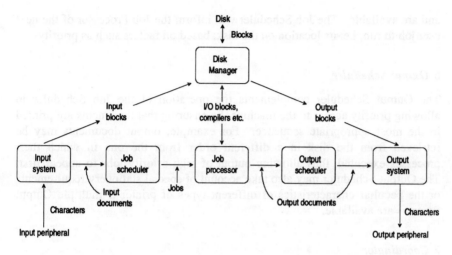

Figure 2.6   Design of a simple spooling system

3 Output System

This process drives the printer through an interrupt procedure. It is responsible for retrieving blocks of a document from the disk, via the Disk Manager, and for transferring the individual characters to the printer. It interfaces with the Output Scheduler whenever a new document is required to be printed.

4 Job Processor

This is the process in which the user program executes. It may be pre-loaded with a range of system utilities to support the user, for example compilers. It will also have procedures which allow the user program to interface with the operating system. For example, read_character and print_character procedures will operate on blocks of input/output documents, brought into buffers in memory by the Disk Manager, and a stop procedure may be called to terminate a program and allow the operating system to run the next user job.

5 Job Scheduler

The Job Scheduler maintains information about all the jobs in the machine waiting to be run, and about the input documents required by the jobs. Its functions are separated from those of the Input System, as potentially many Input System processes may exist to control a number of different input devices, yet only one scheduler is required. User jobs will only become candidates to run when all of their specified input documents have been read and are available. The Job Scheduler will inform the Job Processor of the next user job to run, i.e. its location on the disk, based on factors such as priority.

6 Output Scheduler

The Output Scheduler complements the operation of the Job Scheduler in allowing priority access to the machine, by ensuring that documents are printed in the most appropriate sequence. For example, output documents may be retrieved from the disk in a different order from the one in which their processes executed, thus allowing output of high priority jobs to appear first. The Output Scheduler may also take account of special stationery requirements or the peculiar characteristics of different types of printer if multiple Output Systems are available.

7 Coordinator

The Coordinator is responsible for scheduling the system processes and providing suitable synchronisation mechanisms to allow them to interact. The scheduling itself may be very simple, as rapid process changing within the operating system is essential. Typically two operations will be provided for use by the other processes; a Wait operation which halts the current process and enters the coordinator scheduler, and a Free operation to wake up another process if a service or interaction is required. Further details of scheduling strategies are examined in chapter 4.

2.6 Concepts of time-sharing systems

The simple spooling system is fairly restricted in its applications. Its mode of working, where single jobs or batches of jobs are submitted to the machine and a job is started only when the previous one has been completed, is very effective in achieving good utilisation of the computer system. However, it is definitely not convenient from the user's point of view. The ability to interact with a program is both desirable when developing software and essential for certain types of applications, yet this facility is not available with the spooling system. Most operating systems now provide an interactive capability, and many provide *multi-access* facilities also, where many users are (apparently) able to make simultaneous use of the computer. These rely upon *time-sharing* the resources of the computer between the many users, or to be more precise, between the processes running programs on behalf of the users.

The most important characteristic of a multi-access system is that the computer is reacting to stimuli from a number of devices connected to the machine. The devices may be terminals and the stimulus may be provided by a user typing on the keyboard. However, this is not always the case and, in general, the precise nature of the devices and the ways in which the computer responds are dependent on the application for which the system was designed. It is possible to classify multi-access systems, in broad terms, according to their application, for example real-time/embedded systems, transaction processing systems, and general purpose time-sharing systems.

The general-purpose time-sharing system might be regarded as the normal type of computer system, where users are able to develop and interact with programs online. One form of this, which strictly speaking is not multi-access, is the personal computer or workstation. The more powerful of these allow a single user to have multiple processes operating on their behalf, thereby time-sharing the resources between the tasks of the one user.

Even in its most primitive form, where the terminal is little more than a personalised input/output device, the psychology of interacting directly with the computer rather than relying on operators makes this a far more amenable system, and an immediate indication of 'silly errors' in any interaction, such as control or editing commands, ensures a higher productivity for the user. Most systems allow much more interaction, for example, a user developing software may be able to stop and restart an executing program, set break points, inspect and change variables or step through the program. Again, the emphasis here is on the productivity of the user, in that good facilities for developing new software are provided rather than optimising the use of machine resources. In general, the provision of this type of facility is costly in terms of system efficiency.

The design of a simple time-sharing system is illustrated in figure 2.7. Although the system is primarily supporting terminals, facilities may still be provided for printing documents on a lineprinter or inputting a file or job via a communications link. The input and output spoolers might therefore still be included within the design, although their roles within the system as a whole are now very secondary.

The major feature of this system is that it must be capable of supporting a number of user jobs that are executed (apparently) at the same time. Thus, the module responsible for running the user job (that is, the job processor) has to be replicated for each job in the machine. The time-sharing option is provided by switching the CPU between these job processors as each user demands an interaction with his job. Although effectively there are multiple copies of this job processor module, and each has its own data space, stack and copies of the registers, in practice the code provided within each of the job processors is identical and on some machines a single copy of this code can be shared. This technique is described in chapter 5.

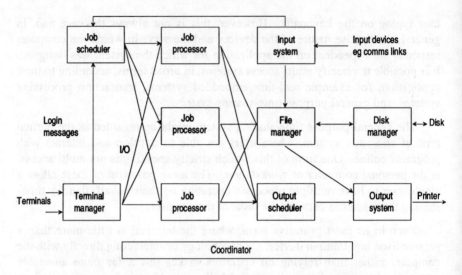

Figure 2.7   Design of a simple time sharing system

The other major differences between this system and the simple spooling system are that facilities must be provided to keep files on the computer and to drive terminals for input/output. A file system is an essential requirement of this system as it is infeasible to input a large document via the input device every time a job is run. This was not the case with the simple spooling system, where large decks of cards could be submitted on every run of a program. However, it is clearly impractical for a user sitting at a terminal to do likewise.

Although it would be possible to integrate the functions of a file manager within the disk manager, logically they are quite different and so it is better to regard them as being in separate modules of the system. The disk manager is primarily concerned with allocating space on the disk and arranging for the data transfers whereas the file manager is more concerned with the management of file directories, the security of files and any associated accounting. The characteristics of the file management software are discussed in chapter 7.

The input and output spoolers in the system might also make use of the facilities provided by the file manager, rather than by communicating directly with the disk manager. By saving input and output documents as files, unprocessed documents can be retained across machine restarts, thus avoiding the need to resubmit jobs whose output had not been printed when the machine was stopped.

The functions of the terminal manager are very different from those of the spoolers that control other input/output devices. Whereas the input spooler might buffer a complete job on the disk before passing information about the document to the job scheduler, the terminal manager will be buffering, in main memory, only single characters or single lines of input data. The first line typed by a user will be sent from the terminal manager to the job scheduler. This will normally identify the user and provide any security checks (password checking) and charging information that may be required as part of the normal sequence for logging-in to the system. The job scheduler assigns a job processor to that particular terminal and informs the terminal manager accordingly. All subsequent input and output operations are then made directly between the terminal manager and the job processor.

2.7 Functional units of a multiprocessor system

Multiprocessing systems relate to the configuration of a computing system with several processors. A schematic of such a system is shown in figure 2.8. The main objective of such systems is to increase throughput by distributing the processing load among the various processing units.

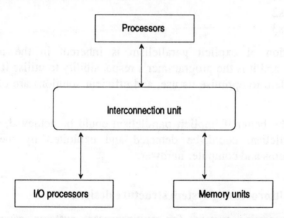

Figure 2.8   A simple multiprocessor organisation

Multiprocessing operating systems have many of the same functions as the multiprogramming systems running on single processors, such as resource allocation and management, data protection, I/O and processor scheduling etc. Detailed discussions of these topics are covered later in this book. For multiprocessing systems, the operating system has to take into account the existence of multiple processing elements, their interconnections and relation-ships. Multiprocessing systems have to consider the issues of reliability, parallelism in computation, optimal interconnection schemes, processor contention and error recovery.

With the existence of multiple processors, it is possible that if a single processor fails, then the remaining ones can continue to function. To achieve this, the operating system needs to detect that a processor has ceased to function and is therefore not available for reallocation as a resource.

Much of the utilisation of multiprocessors relates to the exploitation of the inherent parallelism of computation. It is now possible that there can be sufficient processors so that those operations which can be performed in parallel can be assigned to different processors. The exploitation of parallelism of computation relates both to the hardware and software. This form of exploitation has led to the rapid development of several programming languages, such as occam, Ada and concurrent Pascal, which allow the explicit expression of parallelism. In occam, for example, the PAR construct allows the statements which follow the construct to be executed in parallel, as in the example:

PAR
    process1
    process2
    process3

The exploitation of explicit parallelism is inherent in the programming language used and it is the programmer's responsibility to utilise it. It can be a complex problem to optimise its use, and efficient solutions are often difficult to achieve.

It would be better if implicit parallelism could be achieved, whereby the intrinsic parallelism could be detected and exploited by the compilers, operating systems and computer hardware.

2.8 Some multiprocessing system structure designs

In terms of operating systems for multiprocessor systems, several types of system exist. Three are outlined in this section, namely, master-slave, separate executives and symmetrical systems.

2.8.1 Master-slave

In the master-slave configuration one of the processors is designated the master. This is a general-purpose processor which performs input/output as well as computations. The other processors act as slaves, which perform only computations under the direction of the master processor.

The master-slave system is particularly useful in the situation where there is a great deal of computation with little I/O and where the load is well understood, easy to tune, and scheduling is straightforward. In poorly scheduled jobs there tends to be a queue built up at the master. Any failure of the master will also prove catastrophic to the system as a whole. Some of the problems may be overcome by the use of a looser master-slave coupling whereby the slave has its own operating systems, for example, a network of computers where each one has its own copy of the operating system, but one node has the power to direct the slaves whenever an inter-computer action is required.

2.8.2 Separate executive

In the separate executive system, each processing element has its own operating system and handles interrupts which are generated by user processes running only on itself. Each processor also handles its own I/O devices and files. When a process is assigned to a processor it runs to completion on that processor. I/O devices can be switched between any of the processors but this requires the intervention of a master, or operator operating system. A table of processing elements and the load on each may be maintained globally, but access to such information must be mutually exclusive.

Because each processing element has its own copy of the operating system, there is potential difficulty in resolving conflicts between the processors. This problem is often resolved by the use of voting. In such a system, decisions could be taken on various options, such as majority, or vetoing whereby a single 'no' vote would result in a 'no' decision.

2.8.3 Symmetrical systems

All the processing elements in a symmetrical system are identical and they are managed by an operating system which conceptually 'floats' between the elements. With all the systems being identical, any of them can host the operating system, although only one at a time will be running system activities. This alleviates some of the reliability and resilience problems associated with the master in the master-slave configuration. The process which hosts the system tables and system functionality at any given time is known as the executive processor. At any given instant of time, only one processor can act as executive. Any of the other processors may be used to control any I/O device or to refer to any storage unit. Any process can execute on any of the processor elements and several elements may be combined to cooperate in the execution of any user process.

Conflicts between processors can easily be resolved, depending on the nature of the conflict. In the case of an I/O device or storage unit, the conflict can be handled by hardware. In the case of attempting to access system global information, such conflicts are resolved in the operating system software.

Since there is only one copy of the operating system, conflicts which arose in the case of separate executive systems are avoided. However the code of the operating system must be *re-entrant*, that is it does not change while in use and so will be re-executed in a consistent way. It must also be suitably *mutually exclusive* so that when a processor gains control of a resource, other processors are excluded from accessing it.

Symmetrical systems have the advantage of increased reliability, and in the event of processor failure provide for the possibility of graceful degradation. There is better load balancing of the processors which achieves improved utilisation. However contention problems may be considerable with the possibility of lockout.

In many multiprocessor systems, there is not a linear increase in performance with increasing number of processors. Amongst the factors which reduce the effective utilisation of such systems are additional operating system overheads, increased contention for the system resources, and delays inherent in the switching and routing of transmissions between the various processor elements.

2.9 Summary

The characteristics of modern computer systems often reflect the historical developments which took place during the early days of computing. The need for efficient management of resources, in particular in the use of the CPU, led to the development of spooling systems to offset the speed disparity between processors and i/o devices. It also led to the evolution of multiprogramming systems to enable the overlap of activities, and the development of interrupt systems to allow concurrency of i/o operations and processing. These basic concepts form the heart of modern operating systems, and the terminology originating with those early systems still persists.

This chapter has tracked the development of systems through their evolutionary stages. The concept of a process has been introduced and the structure of an operating system using multiple cooperating processes has been outlined. The design of a simple dedicated spooling system has been described, and the additional requirements of a system to support multi-access and time-sharing have been examined. (A more complete description of such a system is provided in the appendix).

Finally the chapter has reviewed the structure of operating systems for use on multiprocessor machines. Although, in practice, these systems may have additional constraints over their more simple uni-processor counterparts, particularly in terms of their expected resilience and performance, conceptually the operating system processes are very similar and may differ only slightly in their implementation. Other aspects of multiprocessor systems, specifically in a networked context, are examined in chapter 13.

2.10 References and bibliography

P.H. Enslow (1977). 'Multiprocessor Organisation - A Survey', *Computing Surveys*, Vol. 9, No. 1, pp. 103-29.

A.K. Jones and P. Schwarz (1980). 'Experience using Multiprocessor Systems - A Status Report', *Computing Surveys*, Vol. 12, No. 2, pp. 121-65.

T. Kilburn, D.J. Howarth, R.B. Payne and F.H. Sumner (1961). 'The Manchester University Atlas Operating System, Part 1: Internal Organisation', *Computer Journal*, Vol. 4, No. 3, pp. 222-5.

R.W. Watson (1970). 'Timesharing System Design Concepts', McGraw-Hill, New York.

3   I/O Buffering

In chapter 2, simple concepts of input/output (I/O) were described. Because of the differences in speed and signalling level of responses between the CPU and the peripheral devices, there was a need to provide some form of buffering. In this chapter, we review the characteristics of simple buffering systems, identify their deficiencies and consider more sophisticated buffering techniques. Other forms of I/O device handling are also considered, particularly those relating to graphical user interfaces.

3.1 Simple buffering

The behaviour of different forms of I/O management system can be examined based on the premise that a program will take some input, do some processing on it and then generate some output. The unit of input might be single characters, lines of text, transactions or even complete jobs (in which case, our buffering system equates to the spooling systems discussed in chapter 2). A very simple scheme is where processes initiate their input and output operations only when required. This is very inefficient in terms of all resource utilisation, as illustrated in figure 3.1.

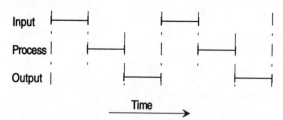

Figure 3.1   Simple device control

It can be seen that the CPU and input/output peripherals do not operate simultaneously, and no attempt is made to overlap the processing of one unit of input with the next. The time to process a unit of input is therefore

input time + process time + output time

Maintaining a simple reservoir or buffer provides the opportunity to exploit concurrency in the operation of the CPU and peripherals, as illustrated in figure 3.2. The input system fills the buffer while the CPU is busy processing the previous unit of input. Thus, when the next unit is required, it can be provided to the process at the speed of the memory rather than the speed of the device. For example, if the unit of input is a complete transaction, the CPU might be processing transaction 1 while the input device is reading transaction 2. Similarly, the CPU will be processing transaction 2 while the results of transaction 1 are being printed.

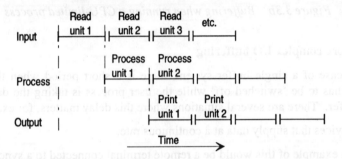

Figure 3.2   Simple buffering to allow overlapped transfers

It can be seen that the utilisation of resources is very much better in this system, although the input, process and output times are rarely so well matched that all resources can be active all of the time. In a steady state, the average time for processing a transaction is

Max (input time, process time, output time)

and the system is quickly reduced to processing transactions at the rate determined by the slowest activity. This can be seen in figure 3.3, which shows the behaviour of the system when running (a) input-limited and (b) CPU-limited processes.

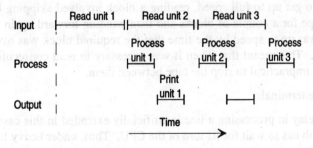

Figure 3.3a   Buffering under input-limited conditions

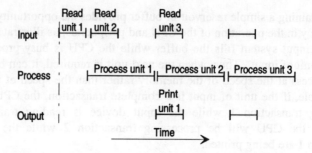

Figure 3.3b   Buffering when running a CPU-limited process

3.2 More complex I/O buffering

In the case of a single buffer system, there is a short period when the input device has to be 'switched off' while the user process is taking the data from the buffer. There are several situations where this delay matters, for example:

(1) Devices that supply data at a continuous rate.

An example of this would be a remote terminal connected to a synchronous line. In this case, the remote terminal determines the transmission rate, and a 'gap' in receiving would mean that data is lost. There is, in this situation, no way of telling the terminal to stop transmitting while the buffer is emptied.

(2) Some magnetic tapes.

Data blocks on the tape are separated by a short, inter-block gap, and it is important that the buffer can be emptied while the read head of the tape deck is traversing this gap. Failure to do so may have differing effects on the performance of the tape system. For example, with some tape drives, the tape will move comparatively slowly due to the repeated application of the braking mechanism. On early tape decks, where the tape took some time to get up to full speed, reading a block involved skipping back down the tape for a couple of blocks and then winding forward again so that the tape was up to speed by the time that the required block was over the read heads. This meant that when it was necessary to read consecutive blocks, it was impractical to stop the tape between them.

(3) Online terminals.

The delay in processing a line is artificially extended in this case when the user job has to wait for its turn of the CPU. Thus, under heavy loading, the response time might be quite long and during this period the user will not be able to continue typing.

A solution to these problems is to use two (or even more) buffers. Thus, after the device has filled one buffer, the user program can be allowed to read from it while the device fills the other, as shown in figure 3.4.

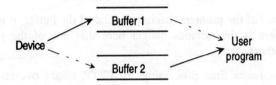

Figure 3.4   Double buffering technique

The buffers are used alternately, with buffer 1 being filled while buffer 2 is being emptied, and vice versa. Provided that the processing rate is faster than the input rate (or the rates are approximately equal), the device can be kept operating continuously.

Before utilising double buffering techniques, some points should be noted:

(1) In a simple system, the processing rate becomes synchronised to the speed of the slowest device and so it is normally only worth while to provide double buffering for the slowest device.

(2) It is not worth while to provide double buffering for any device if the job that controls the devices is CPU-limited.

(3) Double buffering is always worth while if it is inconvenient or expensive to stop a device; for example, where loss of characters would otherwise occur.

The buffering schemes considered so far try to accumulate the data that the user is going to process in a single burst (for example, one line from a terminal). The problem with this is that the length of line varies enormously and, if the maximum value is chosen for the size of the buffer, then in most cases space will be wasted.

One solution is to have a single, fairly large buffer that will hold one or more lines. In general, the buffering process will be placing characters into one end of the buffer while the user is removing them from the other. In effect, the user process is 'chasing' the buffering process down the buffer. This is known as cyclic or circular buffering and is illustrated in figure 3.5 (nl $\equiv$ newline).

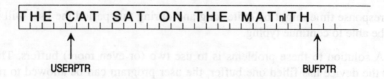

Figure 3.5   Cyclic buffering

When either of the pointers reaches the end of the buffer, it is reset back to the start.   There is the obvious danger here that one of the pointers might overtake the other:

If input is faster than processing, BUFPTR might overtake USERPTR, overwriting data that has not yet been read.

If processing is faster than input, USERPTR might overtake BUFPTR and attempt to read data that has not yet been placed in the buffer.

Obviously, these can be overcome by programming certain checks into the buffering procedures.

Terminal handling provides one of the most common applications for the use of cyclic buffering.   It also illustrates how more sophisticated facilities can be introduced using basically a very simple scheme.   The system used for buffering terminal input has to satisfy the following requirements:

(1) The user process is wakened only when there is a complete line of input for it to process.   There is a significant overhead associated with scheduling a process and this is to be avoided as much as possible. The process is therefore only wakened when the user is expecting a response from the system.

(2) The user must be able to type complete lines of input up to the maximum width of, say, 80 characters.   This determines the minimum size of the buffer.

(3) The user must also be able to correct typing errors on the current line. This involves looking for a logical 'backspace' character (for example, ←).

(4) The user should be able to type more than one line if the system is too busy to process the input instantly.

(5) The user process must be capable of re-reading the line that it is reading.   This enables facilities, such as repeating operations in the editor, to be implemented easily.

(6) A prompt should be output to the user if the system is waiting for input
     and the user has not started typing the next line.

These facilities can be provided using a cyclic buffering system with four
pointers, as in figure 3.6.

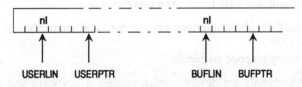

USERLIN   USERPTR   BUFLIN   BUFPTR

Figure 3.6   Cyclic buffering for terminal input

The system has the following characteristics:

(1) The buffer is at least 80 characters long (the length of a line).

(2) Characters are inserted by the buffering process at BUFPTR.

(3) Characters are removed by the user process at USERPTR.

(4) The user process is wakened whenever a newline is placed in the
     buffer.

(5) BUFLIN records the last newline character placed in the buffer. This
     fulfils two functions:

     (a) The user process is halted as soon as USERPTR reaches BUFLIN.
          In addition, a prompt will be output if the user has not typed any
          more input, that is when BUFPTR = BUFLIN.

     (b) The logical backspace facility operates only as far back as
          BUFLIN. This prevents the user from deleting characters that
          have already been read by the process.

(6) USERLIN records the last newline character read by the user process.
     BUFPTR is not allowed to advance past this point, so that the user
     process is always able to re-read the current line.

3.3 Memory mapped systems

Terminals are a standard I/O device for computer systems and they come in a
wide variety of forms. Hardware controllers, or interfaces, act as the
intermediary between the device and the rest of the computer system. It is the
responsibility of a terminal driver to hide the differences between the terminal

forms so that the device-independent part of the operating system and the user program do not have to be rewritten for each type of terminal that is used.

From the point of view of the operating system, terminals can be divided into two broad categories. These are based on the way that the operating system communicates with them. The categories are:

(1) Terminals which interface via standard communication links, such as RS-232
(2) Memory mapped terminals

RS-232 terminals are devices which contain a keyboard and display that communicate using a serial interface one bit at a time. The connection may be many metres in length, so that the terminal itself may be very remote from the computer system. Memory mapped terminals do not communicate with the computer over a serial line. They form an integral part of the computer system itself. These terminals are interfaced via special memory which is called video RAM. This RAM is part of the computer addressable memory space. It can be addressed by the CPU in a similar manner to the rest of the memory space. With the video RAM hardware, there is also a video controller which takes bytes from the video RAM and generates the video signals which are used to drive the display. The video RAM may take two forms, depending on whether the display is solely for characters or a more powerful graphical interface.

From the programmer's point of view, the I/O device appears as a set of registers which can be addressed. Four types of register are typical, namely:

(1) Input data registers
(2) Output data registers
(3) Status registers
(4) Command registers

Input and output data registers are primarily concerned with holding data until the CPU, or the output device, is ready to accept it. Command registers are concerned with transferring I/O commands between the CPU and an I/O device. Status registers are used to provide information to the CPU on the status of the I/O device.

Manipulations concerned with status and command registers are more efficient for memory mapped terminals so that the I/O registers are addressed as memory locations and the instruction set can use the registers as source or destination operands.

For a typical PC monochrome screen displaying up to 80 characters in 25 rows (2000 characters), this uses 4000 bytes of video RAM. When a character is written into video RAM by the CPU it will appear on the screen in one screen display refresh period, namely 0.02 s. The CPU might load a 4 Kbyte pre-computed image into video RAM in 12 ms. In contrast, writing 2000 characters to an RS-232 terminal at a serial communication speed of 9600 bits/s would take 2083 ms, so that the memory mapped terminal is significantly faster.

A typical terminal screen has between 200 and 1200 video lines from top to bottom, with from 200 to 1200 points per line. Each of these points is called a pixel. In a typical monochrome display, a character would be represented in an area which is given by 14 pixels high by 9 pixels wide, so each character written into video RAM would result in the display of a complete block of pixels.

Graphical bit mapped terminals use a principle similar to that of memory mapped terminals except that every bit of the video RAM controls directly a particular pixel on the screen. A typical monochrome screen of 800 by 1024 pixels therefore requires 100 Kbytes of RAM. More memory is required for colour displays, dependent on the number of colours. This system, which provides complete flexibility in character fonts and sizes, makes graphics possible at the level of individual pixels, and allows multiple windows.

3.4 Window management systems

Many terminals now support the use of window management systems, and possibilities of having one or several windows per session exist. A simple model of a window manager is shown in figure 3.7. Applications generate graphics which are to be displayed. A single mouse has to be multiplexed between a number of applications. The operating system under which the window manager is to run will impose constraints both on the window manager and the applications. One of the important considerations is how much of the functionality should be embedded within the operating system itself and how much within other application software and support packages.

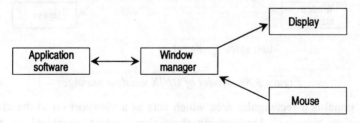

Figure 3.7   Simple window manager

In the case of an operating system such as UNIX, it would seem logical that very little of the window management would be in the operating system kernel. However, because of the inadequate inter-process communication mechanisms and susceptibility to delays in scheduling under heavy load, that system would be unlikely to offer fast enough feedback for a good user interface.

Although it appears attractive to build applications out of a large number of cooperating processes, programs are either in user space and find it hard to communicate with each other, or they are in the kernel in which case they are hard to program and debug. The UNIX window manager therefore is split into two parts one of which is in the kernel and the other in the user space. The window manager cannot be taken completely out of the kernel since there are time-critical tasks such as window update, feedback and mouse control which must be carried out without any delay arising from scheduling, and hence these functions are within the relevant part in the kernel. This means that the part of the manager that deals with the graphics is within the kernel and the part which deals with the user interfacing is within the user space, as shown in figure 3.8. The applications themselves do not see this division.

In this model, the application deals with panels which have no user interface properties, and the kernel resident part of the window manager only knows about panels. The user deals with windows, and all these functions are in the user process.

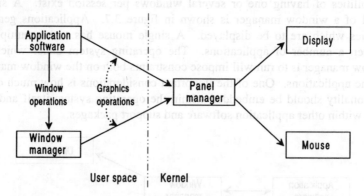

Figure 3.8   Model of UNIX window manager

A panel is a rectangular area which acts as a viewport on to the client or application bitmap. Applications themselves output graphical or textual information to the panels. The interface between the window manager and the panel manager may be at the bitmap level. Applications themselves call graphics primitives in libraries which maintain a bitmap copy of the image which they are displaying. Complete or partial bitmaps are used depending on whether complete panels need to be created or only need partial updating.

Panels have a position and priority, so that they give a division of the screen into a series of possibly overlapping rectangles. They are organised in a hierarchical manner so that each panel has one parent but may have several associated child panels.

Pop-ups menus can be supported by the provision of the menu in a new child panel associated with the appropriate parent panel. This menu can then be deleted by removing the relevant child panel from the hierarchy.

The panel manager, which is the part of the window management system within the kernel, creates and manipulates windows for the user. This manager reserves portions of the panel around the edges and corners to allow the application to access library functions for operations such as scrolling, changing size, moving, etc.

3.5 Summary

This chapter has examined alternative techniques for the management of input/output systems. Historically, the management of i/o systems has been very important and many early operating system designs resulted from the need to achieve good peripheral performance.

I/O operations are fundamental to every operating system, from the large general purpose system down to the embedded system for controlling dedicated applications. Control of peripherals must therefore be approached in an efficient way. Efficiency, in some instances, means being able to keep the peripherals busy all the time without risk of data loss. Various buffering techniques involving single, multiple and cyclic buffers have been developed to support this, and a description of these techniques has been provided in this chapter.

An alternative view of efficiency is centred on the users of systems and the desire to improve user productivity through friendly interactive interfaces. To meet this need, many modern computer systems provide a powerful i/o capability through WIMPs, which enable a user to manipulate icons on a screen via a pointing device such as a mouse. This chapter has therefore provided an overview of the window management systems which are designed to support such an interface.

3.6 References and bibliography

P.J. Denning (1971). 'Third Generation Computer Systems', *Computing Surveys*, Vol. 3, No. 34, pp. 175-216.

S. Rosen (1969). 'Electronic Computers: A Historical Survey', *Computing Surveys*, Vol. 1, No. 1, pp. 7-36.

N. Weizer (1981). 'A History of Operating Systems', *Datamation*, Vol. 1, pp. 119-26.

4   Scheduling

The organisation of the operating system outlined in chapter 2 allows for the time-sharing of the CPU between a number of processes. This technique, however, poses a number of problems; most notably, sharing the available resources between the different job processors. The allocation of resources is the most significant problem faced by an operating system, and one of the most important resource is CPU time. In this chapter, we shall examine the problems of allocating CPU time between the different processes, and some of the basic principles involved in job scheduling.

The main objective of the scheduler is to allocate CPU time to the various processes in such a way as to optimise some aspect of system performance. The main items that we are interested in are:

(1) to provide a good response time
(2) to meet user-specified deadlines
(3) to provide a high CPU utilisation
(4) to provide good utilisation of other system resources

To some extent these are interrelated, with the effect that optimising one of them might degrade the performance of the system with respect to the others. For example, providing a good response time at a terminal will inevitably incur some system overheads, with the effect that overall CPU utilisation is reduced. Thus, scheduling involves a compromise between the various objectives, and the emphasis on each is naturally dependent on the precise nature and use of the system.

4.1 Preemptive and non-preemptive scheduling

Figure 4.1 outlines the organisation of the time-sharing system described in chapter 2. In keeping with the layered or onion model of an operating system, several levels of scheduling are expected within the system, and so far two have been identified: (a) the job scheduler and (b) the coordinator. At the higher level, the job scheduler makes a decision as to which user jobs should be allocated a job processor. It will base its decision on factors such as the loading on the system, i.e. whether a job processor is available, on priority,

41

whether a job has all its input documents available and whether the user has specified any other scheduling advice (for example, a deadline to be achieved). Once a user at a terminal or a job submitted via the input system has been assigned to a job processor, the job scheduler relinquishes all control over the job and scheduling decisions are then performed by the coordinator.

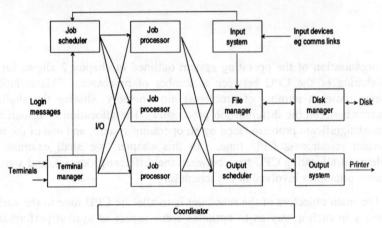

Figure 4.1   Design of a time-sharing system

Now consider the function of the coordinator in a simple system, as shown by the sequence below:

coordinator:

```
REPEAT
    p := 0          {Initialise circular scan of processes}
    REPEAT    {Find a process to run}
        IF process (p) free THEN
            BEGIN
            current proc := p
            restore registers for the process and re-enter process

            {Process P executes . . . and returns by calling wait}

wait:
            save registers
            mark process no longer free
            END
        p := p+1
    UNTIL p > max process number
FOREVER
```

The coordinator selects a process to enter, loads the registers for that process and, in consequence, re-enters the process. This process is run until it waits for an event (such as a disk transfer).

As there is a certain amount of interaction between processes, a facility must be provided so that one process can free another to perform a task for it. This can be achieved with the free procedure in the coordinator, which removes the halted status from the specified process.

    free (p):
        mark process p free
        IF current proc = job processor THEN
            call coordinator

The processes are broadly ordered on priority, so that process(0) is the highest priority and is the first to be examined by the coordinator. However, priority ordering is only applicable in the selection of a process to run. Once it is running, the process is allowed to run to completion (until it calls the WAIT procedure). This is a policy known as *non-preemptive scheduling* and the effect is that, even if a higher priority process is freed, it will not run until the current process has decided to wait.

This policy is acceptable if the processes return control to the coordinator within a reasonable period of time. However, when a user process is involved this cannot be guaranteed and so the coordinator needs to take special action when considering the user process. Thus, in the free procedure, if it is the job processor that is currently running when a process is freed (where the new process, by definition must be of a higher priority), then the job processor is suspended and the coordinator entered. This is a policy known as *preemptive scheduling*.

4.2 Time-slicing

Additional problems occur in time-sharing systems because there are several job processors and each must have the opportunity to use the CPU within the space of a few seconds. The response for a user at a terminal will be unacceptable if their process is waiting much longer than this for a chance to run. Effectively, this means that a user process performing a lot of computing must be *preempted* (that is, have the CPU taken away from it) every few milliseconds to allow other user processes to perform some processing. By this means a process servicing a trivial interaction will receive a rapid response, and processes performing a lot of computing are, of necessity, delayed to let the short ones through.

In order to achieve this type of effect, we need:

(1) Some kind of interrupting clock to trigger the system into making scheduling decisions.

(2) Dynamic adjustment of the priority of processes, so that when a process has had a certain amount of CPU time, others are given preference.

This process of deliberately switching from one process to another on a timed basis is known as *time-slicing*. (The quantum of CPU time allocated to the process is, naturally, known as a *time slice*.)

The act of time-slicing might be performed by the coordinator, although it is probably better to introduce a new module called the process scheduler (or middle-level scheduler) which dynamically adjusts the priorities used by the coordinator. This is done on each timer interrupt. Providing a new module is advantageous for two reasons:

(1) It avoids complicating the coordinator and, as this is the lowest-level scheduler, it is advantageous to keep this as small and efficient as possible.

(2) It enables different kinds of process to be treated differently, for example, some job processors might be processing background work and be exempted from the time-slicing discipline.

Effectively, there are now three levels of scheduling:

High-level scheduler   - Job scheduler
                         Performs the login of a user at a terminal and
                         associates a job processor with the terminal.

Middle-level scheduler - Process scheduler
                         Adjusts the priority of processes and organises time-
                         slicing

Low-level scheduler   - Coordinator
                         Performs logical synchronisation of the processes

Each scheduler has a different perspective of how a job passes through the system. The three schedulers that we have now considered are illustrated in figure 4.2.

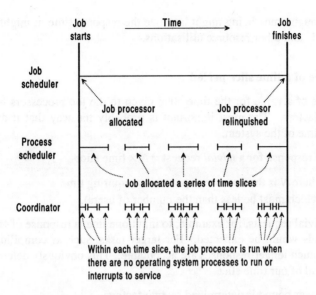

Figure 4.2 Operation of the three schedulers

The use of time slices and the techniques of scheduling so far discussed illustrate how essential preemption is in an online system.   However, preemptive scheduling can be worthwhile even in a purely batch-oriented system. For example, suppose there are two job processors, a high-priority one for short jobs and a low-priority one for long jobs. It is then advantageous to preempt the long jobs in order to get the short jobs through quickly. Consider a system that is mainly running 10-minute jobs, although there are also some 10-second jobs and a non-preemptive scheduling discipline is used; the response for short jobs would be around 5 minutes (the average time to complete the current long job). With preemptive scheduling, the short job would be run first and processed in 10 seconds, while the delay for the long job is not significant unless the number of short jobs is high.

The technique of preemption seeks to provide a better response for the users but it is achieved at some cost in terms of overheads associated with the technique. These overheads are:

(1) The processor time consumed by the system when changing between processes.

(2) The space overheads. With a preemptive system, it is necessary to have a sufficient store to hold all the jobs that are currently in a state of execution. A simple 'one job at a time' system naturally requires less store.

Thus, although time-slicing might improve the response time, it might be at the cost of CPU and other resource utilisations.

4.3 Choice of a time slice period

The choice of a value for the time slice given to the job processors is affected by many factors. The most important is probably the way that it affects the response time of the system.

Worst response for a *trivial* request = $N \times$ time slice

> where N is the number of processes requiring time
> (which must be less than the number of users).

For trivial requests, for example, to input one line, a response of less than 1 or 2 seconds would be expected. For larger tasks, such as compiling a large program, much longer responses are acceptable. This obviously determines the upper bound of our time slice.

The lower bound is determined by two factors:

(1) The overheads of process changing. Transferring jobs to and from memory, register swapping and other coordinator actions all cost time, and the quantum allocated for a time slice should not be so small that these overheads dominate the overall performance.

(2) The quantum should be slightly greater than the time required for a 'typical' interaction. If it is less, then every job will require at least two time slices. For example, consider the case where a typical interaction requires a time of *t*, and a relatively large value has been assigned for the time slice period *s*. Then when a user is allocated a time slice to perform an interaction, the response time seen by the user is as shown in figure 4.3.

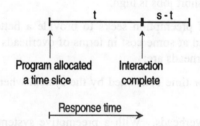

Figure 4.3   Effect of time slice greater than typical interaction

In such a situation, an amount of CPU time equal to (s-t) remains unused from the time slice after the particular interaction has been completed. On the other hand if the time slice period s has a short value that is less than the typical interaction time t, then the response time seen by the user is as shown in figure 4.4.

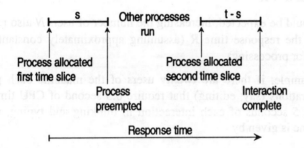

Figure 4.4   Effect of time slice less than typical interaction

The first time slice allocated to the user is not sufficient to complete the interaction and so the user process runs for all that particular time slice. The user program is then preempted and other programs run until the process scheduler allocates a further time slice to this user. In the subsequent interval the user interaction is completed, but it can be seen that the response time for the user has been increased.

In deciding upon a time slice period, a value must be chosen that is at least adequate for servicing a typical user interaction.

4.4 Estimation of response time

In order to estimate the response time of a system, a suitable model must be formulated on which to base the calculations. In practice, this model is very complex because of the nature of the factors that affect it, such as the erratic behaviour of users and the variable overheads of process changing. However, a simple model can be formulated that gives a reasonable approximation to system behaviour, even though it cannot reveal the likely variation in behaviour that a detailed statistical analysis would give.

A simple model can be formed by balancing the amount of 'service' that the system can supply in a given time with the amount being demanded by the users. Clearly, supply must be greater than or equal to demand. (In practice, it would never be equal because of the system overheads associated with scheduling.) Consider a situation where a user is performing, say, an edit command that requires C units of processor time. The user types a command every T seconds and then has to wait a time R before receiving a response back at the terminal. The user therefore requires C units of time every $T + R$ seconds. If there are N users performing similar operations on the machine, they will each be performing a command every $T + R$ seconds, and so

$$N \times C \leq T + R$$

Thus, as would be expected, increasing the number of users N also results in an increase in the response time R (assuming approximately constant times for typing and for processing).

For example, if there are twenty users of the machine each performing similar operations (say, editing) that require 0.5 second of CPU time, and the users spend 5 seconds of each interaction in thinking and typing, an average response time is given by

$$20 \times 0.5 \approx 5 + R$$

Therefore

response time R = 5 seconds

This simple model can be extended to cater for situations when users are not performing similar operations. For example, for students working in a typical teaching laboratory, nineteen short interactions might be needed to edit a file for every long interaction required to compile it. If compiling takes 5 seconds, then every 20 interactions consume

19×0.5 seconds CPU time editing + 1×5 seconds CPU time compiling

If the processes are not subject to time-slicing, then the time for an interaction is still $T + R$ seconds. During the course of twenty interactions, elapsed time can be equated with CPU time allocated, to arrive at the formula

$$20 \times (5 + R) = (19 \times 0.5 + 1 \times 5) \times N$$

which with twenty users gives a response time R of 9.5 seconds. Thus, as would have been expected, injecting longer interactions into the workload results in an increase in the response time.

The behaviour of the system is quite different if the processes are subject to time-slicing. The time to perform a simple interaction will still be $T + R$, where R is now the time that the process is waiting to be allocated a time slice and the time required to perform the necessary operation, for example, an edit command. For the longer interactions, the response time is $T + n \times R$ where n is the number of time slices required to complete the interaction. In the example just considered, for a time slice of 0.5 second, the edit commands are performed in one time slice and the compilations in ten time slices (that is, $n = 10$). Thus, again equating elapsed and CPU time during the course of twenty interactions gives

elapsed time $= 19 \times (5 + R) + 1 \times (5 + 10R)$ seconds

during which time it is still necessary to allocate a CPU time of

$19 \times 0.5 + 1 \times 5$ seconds per process

Consider again a situation where there are twenty users of the machine. Then

$19 \times (5 + R) + 1 \times (5 + 10R) = (19 \times 0.5 + 1 \times 5) \times 20$

or

$R = 6.5$ seconds

Thus, the time for an interaction when editing might be 6.5 seconds and for compiling, which requires ten time slices, the response might be 65 seconds. It can be seen from this that the effect of time-slicing is to reduce the response time for short interactions at the expense of an increased response time for interactions that require several time slices.

4.5 Scheduling algorithms

The approach to be adopted in scheduling depends on the workload of the system and, in particular, on whether the system is (a) deterministic or (b) non-deterministic. The first might include real-time control systems where the frequency at which interactions are required and the processor time required for each is known in advance. The second is the more common and includes general-purpose, time-sharing systems where the user behaviour is more varied. In this case it is necessary to resort to optimising the expected performance using suitable probability distributions for arrival and execution times.

In a deterministic situation, certain features are known about all the tasks to be scheduled, notably: (a) execution time T_i, (b) weighting factor W_i, (c) deadline D_i. From this information, algorithms can be devised for some of the scheduling policies described.

(1) Minimising mean response time.
   Tasks are sequenced in the order of non-decreasing execution time T_i, so that short jobs are favoured in preference to longer jobs.

(2) Minimising mean weighted response time.
   Tasks are sequenced in the order of non-decreasing T_i / W_i, so that the weighting factor W_i takes account of user-specified priority.

(3) Minimising maximum lateness.
   Tasks are sequenced in the order of non-decreasing D_i and, if two tasks have equal deadlines, then they are sequenced in the order of non-decreasing T_i.

(4) Minimising average lateness.
   Although this can be computed, no simple algorithm exists to achieve this.

The behaviour of these algorithms can be demonstrated by considering the scheduling of five tasks whose execution times, weighting factors and deadlines are given below. It is found that the three different scheduling policies yield the following sequences:

i	1	2	3	4	5
T_i	5	6	4	2	3
W_i	1	4	2	3	1
D_i	5	10	15	5	3

(1) Minimum mean response time: T_4, T_5, T_3, T_1, T_2
(2) Minimum weighted response time: T_4, T_2, T_3, T_5, T_1
(3) Minimum maximum lateness: T_5, T_4, T_1, T_2, T_3

These results are immediately available from a single scan of the source data.

This type of scheduling is possible only if the characteristics of the jobs are known in advance. In the case of non-deterministic scheduling, the arrival and execution times for the jobs are not necessarily known. Many algorithms exist, and here a general outline of some of them will be given, namely:

(1) FCFS = First-Come-First-Served
(2) RR   = Round-Robin
(3) SPT   = Shortest Processing Time first
             (non-preemptive)
(4) SRPT = Shortest Remaining Processing Time first
             (preemptive)

First-Come-First-Served (FCFS) scheduling is perhaps the simplest algorithm to implement. Jobs are processed simply in the order in which they are received, without any preemption. This is illustrated in figure 4.5, which shows a queue of jobs arriving in the order A, B, C, D in time. These jobs will then be subsequently processed in the same order, namely A, B, C, D. This means that since it treats all jobs equally, long jobs can hold up short jobs and high and low priority jobs are treated the same. In terms of responsiveness, it gives a small variance of response times. Whilst there is very little overhead on the system, this is not a useful algorithm for scheduling interactive users since it cannot guarantee good response times.

Queue

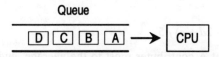

Figure 4.5   First-Come-First-Served Scheduling

Round-Robin (RR) scheduling is preemptive. The jobs are queued in a First-Come-First-Served sequence, and each job is allowed to run for a time slice. At the end of that time slice, if the job is not complete then it is preempted and placed at the back of the queue to await its turn for a subsequent time slice. Short processes may be executed within a single time slice whereas long processes will require several time slices, so that they will have to pass through the ready queue several times before their execution is completed.

The scheduling is illustrated in figure 4.6, where the queue has been formed by jobs arriving in the order A, B, C, D. At the end of the first time slice if job A is incomplete then the order of the queue will become B, C, D, A, assuming that no new jobs have been added to the queue during the time slice. The relative length of the time slice period and the time taken for process switching are important in order to achieve an effective overall performance. Having the time slice period too short will lead to many process switches and lower the CPU efficiency, whereas having a time slice period that is too large will lead to poor response to short interactive requests. The time slice period is usually of the order of milliseconds, and typically is in the range of 1 to 100 milliseconds. RR scheduling is effective in time-sharing situations where it is important to guarantee reasonable response times for interactive users.

Queue

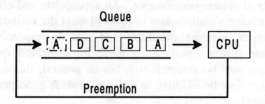

Figure 4.6   Round Robin Scheduling

Shortest-Processing-Time-First (SPT) scheduling is a non-preemptive scheduling algorithm in which the job with the shortest estimated-run time to completion is executed first. This naturally favours short jobs in preference to longer jobs, but minimises the number of jobs waiting behind long jobs. In the case where all the jobs are available simultaneously, then it is possible to prove that SPT is an optimal algorithm for response time. For example, in the case when there are five jobs A, B, C, D, E, with run times a, b, c, d, e respectively, then the average runtime if they are processed in the order A, B, C, D, E is given by

$$(5a + 4b + 3c + 2d + e) / 5$$

where it is clear that A contributes most to the average, and then B, C, and so on, so that if the jobs are ordered in terms of the shortest processing times then they must provide the best average response. In the case shown, the first job will be completed after time a, the second after $a + b$, and so on. The problem is establishing the value of the processing time required to run, which can often only be derived from users' estimates of the length of time required. As in the case of FCFS, this is not a useful algorithm in a time-sharing environment in which reasonable response time must be guaranteed.

Shortest-Remaining-Processing-Time (SRPT) scheduling appears as the preemptive form of SPT. In this case when a new process joins the queue, the scheduler is invoked to compare the remaining CPU of the currently executing process with the time required to complete the next CPU burst of this new process. Depending on the outcome of that comparison, the current process may or may not be preempted. If preemption occurs then the current process returns to the queue. Like the SPT, this scheduling may be proved optimal in the context of minimising the average waiting time. SRPT, which includes preemption, has a higher overhead than SPT, since it must keep track of the elapsed time of the running job and handle the preemption.

4.6 Summary

Scheduling the workload of a computer system must take into account the different aspects of system performance. An appropriate and efficient strategy may therefore involve a compromise in order to meet the various constraints of resource utilisation, meeting deadlines and overall responsiveness of the system. In some systems, particularly those for dedicated applications, the optimum solution may be deterministic, but in general, this is not the case. Systems must therefore be adaptive in order to provide good performance (but with no guarantees).

This chapter has examined a number of scheduling strategies, involving algorithms for both deterministic and non-deterministic systems. The use of preemption as a scheduling mechanism has also been discussed. The most common preemptive mechanism involves time-slicing the processes so that each receives a small amount of CPU time before it is forced to relinquish control of the CPU. The time-slicing mechanism has been described, including the factors which affect the choice of time-slice period.

4.7 References and bibliography

R.B. Bunt (1976). 'Scheduling Techniques for Operating Systems', *Computer*, Vol. 9, No. 10, pp. 10-17.

E.G. Coffman and P.J. Denning (1973). *'Operating Systems Theory'*, Prentice-Hall, Englewood Cliffs, New Jersey.

L. Kleinrock (1975). *'Queuing Systems, Vol II: Computer Applications'*, Wiley-Interscience, New York.

S. Lauesen (1975). 'Job Scheduling Guaranteeing Reasonable Turnaround Times', *Acta Informatica*, Vol. 2, No. 1, pp. 1-11.

M. Ruschizka and R.S. Fabry (1977). 'A Unifying Approach to Scheduling', *Communications of the ACM*, Vol. 20, No. 7, pp. 469-77.

5 Memory Management - Basic Principles

The allocation of memory to the processes in a time-sharing system poses one of the most major problems to designers of operating systems. If the system is supporting a large number of user processes, say N, in general it is impractical to keep all of them in memory, as on average only $1/N$ of the store will be in use at any given instant. Apart from the process that is currently running, some processes will be waiting for a time slice and some (usually the overwhelming majority) will be waiting for a response from the user. This latter category is the most problematic, as the typical response that can be expected from the user might be of the order of a few seconds (but might even be hours). Clearly, the system should not allow such a valuable commodity as its main memory to be under-utilised to such an extent.

In most time-sharing systems, this problem is overcome by a technique known as swapping:

Inactive processes are kept on the backing store in the form of a *store image*. Whenever the user interacts and is expecting a response, the process is allocated a time slice and the store image is loaded into memory before the process is restarted. On completion of the time slice, or when the process is waiting for the user to respond again, the store image may be transferred back to the backing store.

The backing store, often referred to as the secondary storage, may in practice consist of a hierarchy of storage devices, varying in capacity and speed from comparatively small, fast fixed head disks, to slow but larger exchangeable disks or similar mass storage devices. Similarly, the main memory, or primary storage, may be augmented by high-speed cache stores. In a typical system, the memory management software might have to organise the swapping of programs between any of these levels in the storage hierarchy, although the management of the cache stores is in general a function of the hardware.

Irrespective of the number of levels in the storage hierarchy, the principles involved in swapping are the same as if only a single backing store and main memory existed. This two-level structure will therefore be assumed when considering memory management techniques.

Swapping naturally incurs an overhead and so great care is needed as to when to transfer a program into or out of memory. For example, simple input/output operations to the terminal may be buffered by the operating system, thus avoiding having to keep the process in memory while the user is typing.

5.1 Swapping strategies

There are several variations in technique for swapping programs. These may vary in (a) the total amount of memory required and (b) the time lost as a result of swapping. In particular, this latter factor may have a constraining effect on the number of terminals that can be serviced with a reasonable response time. To illustrate this, the behaviour of a number of different swapping strategies will be considered.

5.1.1 Simple swapping system

The simplest case would be a system where the main memory is large enough for just the operating system and a single user process, and all processes have to be swapped into the single space when they are allocated a time slice. This situation is illustrated in figure 5.1.

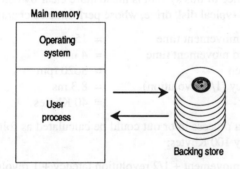

Figure 5.1   Simple swapping system

The criteria used for assessing the swapping strategy, namely the memory and speed requirements, show:

memory size = 1 process + operating system
time for each interaction   = swap in time + CPU time + swap out time
                                    = 2 × swap time + CPU time

The CPU time will vary according to what the process is doing, up to a maximum value given by the time slice period.

Assessing the efficiency of this system as

$$\frac{\text{useful time}}{\text{total time}} \times 100 \text{ per cent}$$

then

$$\text{CPU utilisation} = \frac{\text{CPU time}}{2 \times \text{swap time} + \text{CPU time}} \times 100 \text{ per cent}$$

The performance of this system is quite clearly dependent on the behaviour of the user process and the amount of CPU time it actually consumes whilst swapped into memory for its time slice. If the CPU time needed to process an interaction is quite short, the formulae show that there is a poor CPU utilisation but quite a rapid response for the user, with the swap time being the dominant factor. It is worth noting that this is one of the most major problems with time-sharing systems, where highly interactive jobs result in a low overall CPU utilisation.

For interactions that require a large amount of CPU time, such as running a large compilation, the CPU utilisation is naturally much better. However, it is still dominated by the swap time, as the processes have to be time sliced in order to guarantee a reasonable response time.

The performance of this system is made more clear by considering in detail the behaviour of a typical disk drive, whose performance characteristics are:

average head movement time	= 15 ms
minimum head movement time	= 4 ms
rotational speed	= 3620 rpm
average latency (1/2 revolution)	= 8.3 ms
capacity/track	= 40 Kbytes

The time to swap a process in or out could be calculated as follows, assuming a process size of, say 100 Kbytes:

average head movement + 1/2 revolution latency + 1 revolution transfer
(for first track)
+ minimum head movement + 1/2 revolution latency + 1 revolution transfer
(for each subsequent track)

= 15 + 8.3 + 16.6	(first track reading 40 Kbytes)
+ 4 + 8.3 + 16.6	(next track, also 40 Kbytes)
+ 4 + 8.3 + 8.3	(final track of 20 Kbytes)
= 81.4 ms	

A typical time slice period on such a system might be 100 ms, and so:

total time for an interaction $= 2 \times 81.4 + 100$ ms
$= 262.8$ ms

If the system had to guarantee a response time of less than 2 seconds, then it could support 8 users on the machine at once. This is quite low, and indeed, the overall efficiency of the CPU is only:

CPU utilisation $= \dfrac{100}{263} \times 100$ per cent

≈ 38 per cent

Even this estimation is somewhat optimistic as it assumes that each process will use its 100 ms slice of computing time. If the interaction takes less time than that, the utilisation will be even worse.

5.1.2 A more complex swapping system

The disadvantage with the simple swapping system is that the CPU is idle whilst a process is being transferred in and out of memory, and even with CPU-limited jobs and a comparatively large time slice period, the swap time is still the dominant factor. The natural development to alleviate this problem is to try to overlap some of the swapping with the computing in another user process. For this, the system has to be able to hold more than one process in memory at a time, as illustrated in figure 5.2.

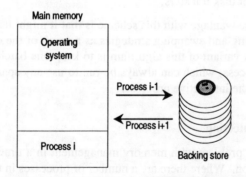

Figure 5.2   A more complex swapping system

With this scheme, process *i* executes while the previous process (process *i*-1) is swapped out and the next (process *i*+1) is swapped in. This system relies on the process executing for a time sufficient to swap one process out and another one in, and indeed, the maximum value assigned for a time slice period might be aimed at achieving this balance.

5.1.3 Further developments of the swapping system

The more complex swapping system still has the disadvantage that its performance is dependent on the single user process that is currently in memory. If this does not use its full time slice, as is very probable with highly interactive jobs, the performance of the system is dominated by the times taken to go to and from the backing store. An extension of this system is therefore to provide for a number of processes to be in memory waiting to run (the precise number is arbitrary, but still considerably less than the total number in the system). The following strategy can then be adopted:

(1) If a process waits for input/output, then it is likely to be waiting for several seconds before the next line is typed in and so it can be swapped out immediately.

(2) If a process is preempted because its time slice has run out, it is preferable to retain it in store. There is a good possibility that the process will be scheduled and run again without needing to reject it from memory. In addition, if the later processes do not use their full slice of CPU time, it might be possible to switch to those left in memory to utilise the spare capacity. There is also a reduction in the loading of the disk channel owing to the elimination of wasteful and redundant disk transfers.

The main disadvantage with this scheme is that it might lead to some quite complex scheduling and swapping strategies as a result of the close interaction between them. A variant of this algorithm is to keep one batch job in store (as a background process) which can always be run to use any spare CPU capacity whilst swapping the interactive processes.

5.2 Memory protection

The second main problem with memory management in a time-sharing system is one of protection. Where there are a number of processes in the machine, the operating system has to protect each from interference by the others, not forgetting, of course, that it also has to protect itself from interference by the user programs. A number of techniques exist for protecting the resources in the system from illegal access by user programs. The more advanced techniques for this will be considered in chapter 10. In this chapter, the main consideration will be techniques specifically concerned with protecting storage.

In practice, the problem of protecting the operating system from a user is basically the same as protecting one user program from another.

In the simple system shown in figure 5.3, the user process is placed in memory at location 0 and the operating system at the top of memory. When the user job is running, it should be able to access only locations O to N, whereas when the operating system is running, addresses up to the memory size S should be permitted.

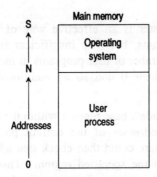

Figure 5.3   A simple memory organisation

The validity of addresses has to be checked by hardware as it must be performed on every memory access and special hardware is the only efficient way of achieving this. If it is assumed that the operating system is trustworthy and so there is no need to check the addresses generated by it, the only check that must be applied is that no address greater than N is generated when in a user program. For the hardware to apply this check, it must know two items:

(1) Where the operating system starts, that is N (a special register could be used to hold this information).

(2) Whether the user program or the operating system is running at any instant in time.

The most common way of implementing this is by providing two modes of execution, a *user mode* and a *privileged mode*. In user mode, only addresses 0 to N are valid, whereas in privileged mode, addresses 0 to S are permissible. The transition from user mode to privileged mode is performed either:

(1) When an interrupt occurs, at which time the value of the program counter is also set to an entry point in the operating system code.

(2) As the result of a special 'enter operating system' instruction.

Thus, privileged mode is set only when obeying operating system code.

Attempts to access non-existent locations or addresses in the operating system when in user mode result in a program fault interrupt. The interrupt entry sequence sets privileged mode and also sets the program counter to the start of an interrupt procedure in the operating system. Other program fault conditions have a similar effect, as do certain kinds of instructions, such as HALT, which are deemed to be illegal in user mode.

5.3 Virtual addressing

The use of a limit register is an effective way of protecting the operating system from user programs, but it is insufficient in a general time-sharing system. If there are a number of user programs in memory, it is impossible to start all of them at address 0 and so an additional mechanism within the hardware is necessary.

One option is to include a base register within the hardware so that both the starting and finishing addresses of the current program are known. The memory accessing hardware could then check that addresses generated by the user programs lie within the specified region. This provides the necessary protection but has a number of significant drawbacks. If the operating system is time-slicing the programs and swapping them in and out of memory, it is very inconvenient (and inefficient) if programs have to be loaded into precisely the same physical locations that they occupied on the previous time slice. Although programs may be compiled to be relocatable, it is not feasible to try to relocate a 'store image' at a different address at the start of each time slice.

The most satisfactory solution is to provide the relocation mechanism within the memory accessing hardware itself. Each process therefore sees a *virtual store* or *virtual memory* that extends from address 0 up to some limit *N*. In practice, the program may reside in the real memory starting at address *B*, as shown in figure 5.4.

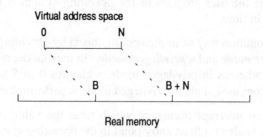

Figure 5.4   Virtual store mapping

The translation between virtual and real addresses has to be performed for every memory access in user mode, and this can be performed efficiently only if suitable hardware is provided between the CPU and the store. The most simple form of hardware for doing this translation is the base-limit register system shown in figure 5.5.

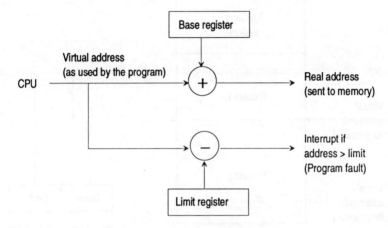

Figure 5.5   Base-limit register

Prior to entering a process, the coordinator sets the base register to the start of the memory allocated to it and the limit register to its size. This would be performed as part of the register reloading sequence executed normally when entering a process. When in user mode, all addresses are translated by adding the base register to the virtual address generated by the program. This produces a real address which is sent to the memory.

A check is also made for addresses outside the permissible range of the program by comparing the virtual address with the limit register. If the virtual address is greater, then an interrupt is generated and the operating system entered to perform suitable remedial action (such as faulting the program or allocating more space).

The memory organisation of a typical system is illustrated in figure 5.6. Here, the time-sharing system is supporting a number of user processes, each with its own virtual address space starting at virtual address 0, but not constrained to any particular real address.

The action of the memory accessing hardware when the machine is in privileged mode varies between different computers. On some, an alternative set of address translation registers is provided for the system software, in effect providing the operating system with its own virtual address space. On other

machines, the address translation mechanism is bypassed altogether so that the
operating system uses real addresses.

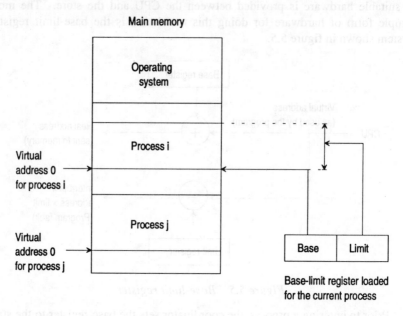

Figure 5.6   Memory management in a base-limit register system

5.4 Segmentation

So far in this chapter, the memory management system described provides an
adequate set of facilities for implementing a reasonable time-sharing system.
Each user process has its own virtual store which is protected from interference
by other processes by the use of the base-limit register. Additionally, this
mechanism protects the operating system from illegal accesses by the user
programs.   Many early computers relied solely on this technique for
implementing a suitable multi-access system, but there are still a number of
major problems outstanding for the system designer, most notably: (a)
fragmentation, (b) locality of programs and (c) sharing of data structures or
code, such as compilers and editors. Each of these will now be considered.

5.4.1 Fragmentation

The problem of fragmentation (or more specifically, external fragmentation)
stems from the fact that processes are continuously being swapped in and out of
memory. The sizes of the processes vary with the effect that when a process is

transferred out, a space is left in memory which is of a variable size. Similarly, when transferring a process into memory, a space must be found which is sufficient for it to fit into. The memory is said to be fragmented if the free space is split into many small areas, and as a consequence there is a situation where

total free space > program size

yet there is no contiguous space large enough to hold the new program.

Fragmentation is largely dependent on the techniques used to maintain a pool of free space, and the allocation from this pool. For example, consider the following strategies:

(1) A single empty space could be maintained at the top of memory by shuffling the programs down whenever a hole is created. This would completely eliminate the problem of fragmentation but is very time-consuming as a lot of information may need to be transferred at the end of each time slice. This becomes increasingly ineffective if the size of the computer system (and correspondingly the main memory) is large.

(2) The system might keep a list of free blocks (and their sizes), and the allocation algorithm might then allocate, say, the first hole it finds greater than the required size. If there is not a space large enough, the technique might then resort to strategy (1). Alternatively, the allocation algorithm might be made more selective by allocating the smallest space which is large enough for the program. The idea behind this is to leave the biggest holes untouched. A consideration of these and other algorithms is presented in chapter 8.

(3) The programs already in memory could be run until one of them finishes and leaves a large enough space. However, this might seriously affect the response time of the system through giving some programs an unduly long time slice.

Although fragmentation has only been considered in the context of allocating space in the main memory, it should be remembered that exactly the same problems can occur when allocating space on the backing store.

5.4.2 *Program locality*

Program locality is largely concerned with the way programs use their virtual address space. Although the address space is uniform, that is all store locations have similar characteristics, the pattern of accesses to these store locations is far from being uniform. This gives rise to two main areas of inefficiency: (a) static sparseness and (b) dynamic sparseness.

(a) Static sparseness

The real storage allocated must be equivalent to the range of virtual addresses used, even though the program might be using the space very sparsely.

Figure 5.7 illustrates a case in point, where a program has its code residing at one end of the virtual store and its data structures at the other. Unfortunately, real storage has to be allocated to cover the space between, even though the program might never access it. There is also an extra time overhead to be suffered when swapping the program into memory with having to transfer the redundant information.

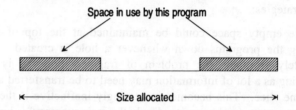

Figure 5.7   Sparse usage of the virtual address space

An immediate reaction might be that this was bad programming practice and that users who programmed in this way deserved poor efficiency from their computer system. However, consider how a compiler might arrange its data structures in store. This is illustrated in figure 5.8.

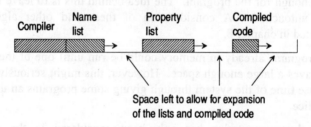

Figure 5.8   Possible memory organisation during compiling

The compiler must assign space for its data structures assuming that it is compiling a very large program. Of course, with small programs most of the space assigned for the name list, property list, etc. will be unused. However, this is unavoidable unless an optimised compiler is provided specifically for small programs.

(b) Dynamic sparseness

The information accessed by a program during a time slice is often quite small. For example, the program might be running within a single procedure, operating on only one or two of its data structures. However, *all* of the program and data must be brought into store on *every* occasion. This situation is known as dynamic sparseness and is illustrated in figure 5.9.

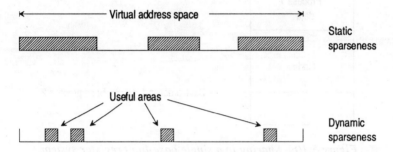

Figure 5.9   Comparison of static and dynamic sparseness

5.4.3 Sharing of code and data

A number of cases have already been encountered where there is a logical need for programs to share store. For example, in the time-sharing system outlined in chapter 4, communication between the various system processes may take place through data structures in shared memory. There are also cases when it would be beneficial to be able to share code. For example, in a time-sharing system where there are a number of processes using the same compiler, the ability to share a single copy of the compiler's code between all programs has a significant and beneficial effect on both the total memory occupancy and the swap times, as there is no need to swap a copy of the compiler in and out with each process.

In order to be able to share programs, they must be expressed as *pure code*, that is: (a) the program is not self-modifying in any way, (b) the data is kept separately from the program (and probably accessed via one or more registers which can be given different values in different processes). Quite clearly, a program that modifies itself cannot be shared, and neither can one whose data areas cannot be made different for each of the processes that use it.

Sharing in a controlled and protected way is extremely difficult to achieve in a single base-limit register machine. Consider, for example, the situation shown in figure 5.10.

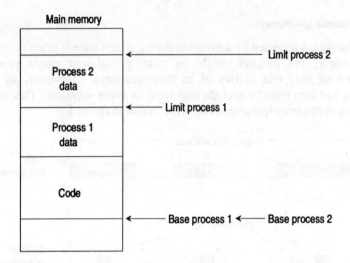

Figure 5.10   Sharing in a single base-limit register system.

In this case, code is being shared between two processes, each having its own data area. Although the base-limit register can be set for process 1 to restrict its address space to the code and its own data area, we are unable to do the same for process 2. This relaxation of the protection system might be permissible if the two processes are part of the operating system (and hence are tried and trusted). However, it is clearly unacceptable in the general case when user programs are needing to share code.

5.4.4 Multiple base-limit register machines

The three problem areas of fragmentation, sparseness and sharing together have a serious impact on the overall structure and efficiency of a time-sharing system. For this reason, most modern machines supporting large multi-access systems rely on alternative forms of memory management to help alleviate these difficulties.

In the case where information is shared between programs, there is an obvious way in which changes to the hardware can improve the situation. If there are two base-limit registers in the hardware, one can be used for translating the addresses for accesses to the code and the other for accesses to the data areas, as shown in figure 5.11. The hardware is aware of which register to use for address translation at any instant, as the control logic knows whether an instruction is being fetched or an operand being accessed.

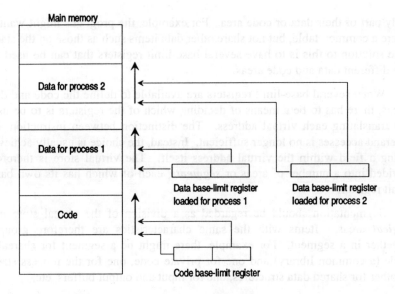

Figure 5.11a   Sharing of code between processes

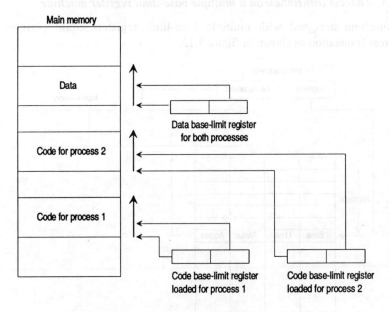

Figure 5.11b   Sharing of data between processes

This provides an effective means of sharing either the data area or the code area. It still has some deficiencies, however, as programs may want to share only part of their data or code area. For example, the programs might want to share a common table, but not share other data items such as those on the stack. The solution to this is to have several base-limit registers that can be used for the different data and code areas.

When several base-limit registers are available to define the code and data areas, there has to be a means of deciding which of the registers is to be used for translating each virtual address. The distinction between instruction and operand accesses is no longer sufficient. Instead, the choice is usually achieved using a field within the virtual address itself. The virtual store is therefore divided into a number of areas or *segments*, each of which has its own base-limit register.

Segmentation should be regarded as a division of the virtual store into *logical* areas. Items with the same characteristics are therefore grouped together in a segment. For example, there might be a segment for shareable code (a common library) and one for private code, one for the process stack, another for shared data structures, one for input and output buffers, etc.

5.4.5 Address translation on a multiple base-limit register machine

A machine designed with multiple base-limit registers could perform its address translation as shown in figure 5.12.

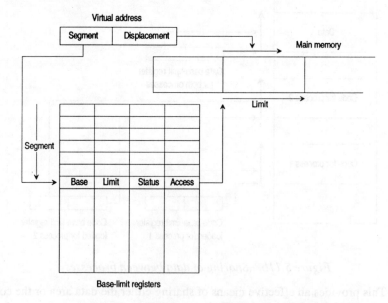

Figure 5.12   Multiple base-limit register system

A virtual address, as used by a program, is split into two parts. The segment field indexes into a table of base-limit registers. Once a register is selected in this way, the operation is similar to that in the single base-limit register system. The displacement part of the virtual address is added to the base to give the required real address. It is also checked against the limit of the register to ensure that the program does not try to access locations beyond the allocated size of the segment.

There are several important features about this system that influence the operating system design and its overall behaviour.

(1) The operating system maintains a *segment table* for each process that holds the base-limit values for each of the process segments. On process changing, the hardware base-limit registers are loaded from the segment table of the process being entered. On some machines this has to be performed by software, that is by the coordinator as part of the register reloading sequence for the program. On other machines, loading of the registers is performed by the hardware when a special register, known as the *Segment Table Base Register* is assigned the starting address of the segment table. On such machines, the layout of the operating system tables must conform with the format expected by the address translation hardware.

(2) As each segment has its own limit register, the amount of space allocated for mapping the virtual store can be restricted to a minimum. The system no longer needs to allocate memory to cover the unused areas in the virtual store and so the problem of static sparseness is resolved. In the extreme, some segments may even have a limit of zero, that is, be completely unallocated.

(3) The segment table entries might point to segments resident on the backing store. The operating system might then bring the segments into memory only when they are accessed. This is known as *demand loading* and obeys the following sequence:

   (a) A program attempts to access a particular segment but the attempt fails as the status field in the base-limit register shows that the segment is not in memory.

   (b) A *virtual store interrupt* is generated and the operating system is entered with information about the required virtual address.

   (c) The operating system decodes the virtual address, loads the segment into memory and changes the segment table (and base-limit register) accordingly.

(d) The program is restarted, re-executes the instruction that previously failed and proceeds.

This partially solves the problem of dynamic sparseness as only segments currently being accessed need be loaded into memory. It is not a complete solution, however, as the whole segment has to be loaded even though accesses may be very localised.

(4) As it is unnecessary to load *all* of a program into memory at the same time, a much larger virtual store can be allowed than there is real store available. For example, many 32-bit machines allow a virtual address space of 2^{32} bytes. This is clearly much larger than the main store available on any machine. Naturally, if a program tries to access all of its virtual store at once, it cannot all fit into the main memory, and so segments may be swapped into and out of memory by the operating system while running the program.

(5) Division of a program into logical units allows much better protection to be provided for the individual segments. In particular, it is possible to protect against faulty accesses, such as write accesses to the code segments. This is implemented with the aid of additional access permission bits in the base-limit registers. The permission field is checked on each store access to ensure that the required type of access is allowed. There might typically be at least three bits signifying:

read	reading of operands allowed
write	write to operands allowed
obey	instruction fetch accesses allowed

A fourth permission bit is often provided to distinguish segments in the virtual store that are accessible only to the operating system.

The use of these access permission bits again emphasises that segmentation is a logical division of the virtual store, where items with similar characteristics and access modes are grouped together. For a simple program, such as an editor, there might be segments for:

code	obey only (or obey and read)
input file	read only
output file	read and write
stack	read and write

The operating system might also keep a fifth permission bit in the segment table entries. This is not accessed by the hardware but indicates whether a user is allowed to change the access permission associated with the segment.

5.4.6 Shared segments

Division of the virtual store into segments opens up a convenient and logically clean way of sharing information between processes, as individual segments can be shared without reducing the protection that each process expects for the rest of its virtual store. The organisation of the operating system tables still presents a problem to the system designer, as there are at least three distinct ways in which the tables can be structured. These will be identified as: (a) all direct, (b) one direct, all others indirect, (c) all indirect.

The choice of technique for any particular system might depend to a large extent on the hardware support for reloading the base-limit registers, as well as on other performance constraints.

(a) All direct

In this scheme, as shown in figure 5.13, the processes sharing the segment each have their own segment table entry with a copy of the base-limit values for the segment.

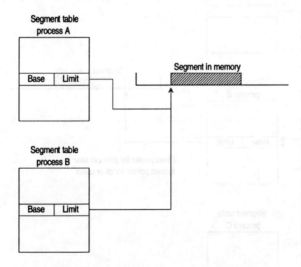

Figure 5.13   Shared segments, all direct

There are certain features of this system worth noting:

(1) The segment number does not need to be the same in each user's virtual store. For example, segment 1 in process A might be the same as segment 3 in process B.

(2) A complication arises if the segment has to be moved (for example, swapping it into and out of store) as all of the segment tables pointing at it must be altered accordingly. This leads to complicated list structures where the segment tables are linked together. In some respects, therefore, it is not a good technique, as it incurs significant run-time overheads in maintaining the system tables.

(b) One direct, all others indirect

In this system, shown in figure 5.14, the principal user has a direct pointer (a base-limit value) from its segment table to the required segment in memory. Other processes have to use indirect pointers from their segment tables into the segment table of the principal user, and thence indirectly access the relevant segment in memory. In this case, note that:

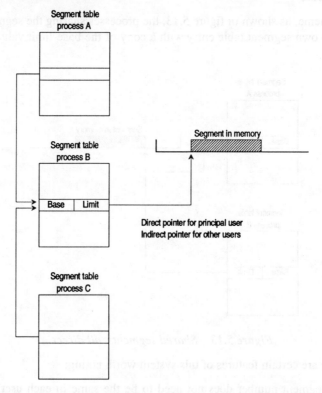

Figure 5.14   Shared segments, one direct, all others indirect

(1) An indirect bit is required in the segment table entries to determine whether the entry is pointing directly at the segment or at another segment table entry. If the base-limit registers are loaded by hardware, this additional status bit will need to be recognised by the address translation mechanism.

(2) This scheme is satisfactory if the owner of the segment is permanent, but situations may arise where the system needs to move the segment table for the owner (such as between time slices when the process is otherwise dormant), or where the owning process terminates or when it is necessary to delete the segment from the virtual store.

(c) All indirect

The system involving only indirect pointers to shared segments is shown in figure 5.15. This seeks to improve on the deficiencies found in the previous system by maintaining a separate table for the shared values of the base-limit registers. This table is often called either the *global segment table* or the *system segment table*.

Although it is possible to use the system segment table only for segments which are shared, and otherwise to use direct pointers in the process segment tables, it is usually more convenient, and simple, if the system segment table holds details of *all* base-limit register addresses known to the system. Each process has its own *local segment table* and this provides a pointer into the system segment table from which the relevant base-limit information can be obtained. A segment is shared by having identical pointers. In this case:

(1) If the segment is moved, only one table, namely the system segment table, needs to be altered.

(2) The system segment table defines all the segments known to the operating system. The index into this table (the system segment number SSN) therefore provides a unique identification for the segment. This is often used elsewhere within the operating system when referring to the segment.

(3) The system segment table is *never* moved, so there is no difficulty with updating the pointers from the individual local segment tables.

(4) The local segment table entries hold the access permission that each user has to the segments. As a result, users can have different access permissions to the same segment. For example, one user may have read and write access permission; a second (less-trusted user) may only be able to read the segment.

(5) The base-limit value is in the system segment table so that users sharing a segment share *all* of the segment. This again is in keeping with the notion of a segment being a single logical entity and, as such, each segment is indivisible.

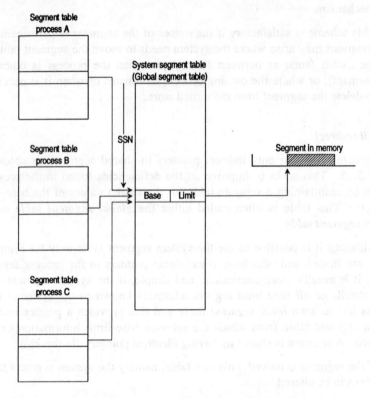

Figure 5.15   Shared segments, all indirect

A rather special case of sharing information concerns the provision of frequently used software for user programs, such as editors, compilers, mathematical and graphics libraries etc. It is possible to make these readily available in the user's virtual store by preloading each process segment table with entries for segments containing the utilities. However, this is wasteful as the same information would be duplicated for all user processes.

An alternative solution is to have a separate *common segment table*, which has a similar structure to the local segment tables associated with each process. Segment numbers above a certain predefined value (for example, the top half of the virtual address space) are then translated via this rather than the local tables. In addition to saving space within the system data structures, this technique may also have performance benefits, as the loading of base-limit registers need not be performed for these segments on a process change. This structure is also recognised within the hardware of some computer systems, which provide two segment table base registers, one for the local segment table and one for the common segment table.

5.5 Summary

This chapter has examined the problems that arise when multiple processes co-exist in memory. The overheads of swapping processes to and from the disk have been calculated based on typical disk performance characteristics and program size. This revealed a clear need to keep as many processes in memory as possible in order to achieve reasonable CPU utilisation and response time. However this also introduces the problems of relocating processes, as they may reside at different memory addresses each time they are scheduled, and of protecting processes so that any one process cannot interfere with the memory of another (or of the operating system). Solutions to both of these are discussed, using virtual addressing techniques.

The use of a single base-limit register provides a simple means of implementing virtual addressing. However the technique suffers from a number of difficulties, namely fragmentation of memory, inefficiency due to program locality (static and dynamic sparseness) and inadequate means of sharing memory when necessary. A segmented virtual store resolves some of these problems by partitioning the memory into a number of logical units or segments. Static sparseness is no longer problematical as demand loading of segments whenever required ensures that only useful information is allocated space and transferred into memory. Segments also provide an effective unit of sharing. The use of multiple base-limit registers for implementing segment-ation and alternative strategies for sharing segments have been described.

The resolution of some memory management problems, and in particular fragmentation, are still open issues which will be addressed in chapter 6.

5.6 References and bibliography

C. Bays (1977). 'A Comparison of Next-fit, First-fit and Best fit', *Communications of the ACM*, Vol. 20, No. 3, pp. 191-2.

J.B. Dennis (1965). 'Segmentation and the Design of Multiprogrammed Computer Systems', *Journal of the ACM*, Vol. 12, No. 4, pp. 589-602.

C.A.R. Hoare and R.M. McKeag (1972). 'A Survey of Store Management Techniques', *Operating System Techniques*, Academic Press, London, pp.117-51.

A.W. Madison and A.P. Batson (1976). 'Characteristics of Program Localities', *Communications of the ACM*, Vol. 19, No. 5, pp.285-94.

B. Randell (1969). 'A Note on Storage Fragmentation and Program Segmentation', *Communications of the ACM*, Vol. 12, No. 7, pp. 365-72.

6 Memory Management - Paging Algorithms and Performance

In chapter 5 it was shown how the multiple base-limit system evolved in an effort to solve the problems inherent in the single base-limit register system. The problems of sharing and sparseness have largely been resolved, although in the case of dynamic sparseness the solution is not entirely satisfactory as whole segments have to be transferred in and out of memory in order to access just a single location. However, there are still problems with the segmented system, namely: (a) fragmentation and (b) a potential deadlock situation when a number of processes are being multiprogrammed, since, although all the processes have some of their segments in memory, the number may not be enough to run (or at least to run efficiently).

6.1 Paging

The problem of fragmentation arises because storage space is allocated in variable sized units. The solution, in simple terms, is to allocate memory only in fixed sized units. This concept is known as *paging*, where the user's addressing space is split into a number of pages of equal size. Although this division is not immediately apparent to the user, the virtual address must be structured in order to allow mapping of the pages on to the real store. The address translation mechanism therefore assumes a format for the virtual address as shown in figure 6.1.

Page	Displacement

Figure 6.1   Virtual address space

This division should not be confused with that seen with segmentation. Segmentation was defined to be a *logical* division of the virtual store, where the segments could be of a variable size and with different protection attributes. Thus, a segment might contain a complete text file or a compiler. Paging is a *practical* division of the store, intended primarily to avoid the problems of fragmentation. The pages are of a fixed size, and are usually considerably smaller than the size normally required for segments.

77

The main disadvantage with paging is that space may be wasted if only very small areas of store are required, as the smallest unit that can be allocated is a page. This problem is known as internal fragmentation, and its main effect is on the choice of the page size for a machine.

6.1.1 Address translation in a paged machine

The mapping of virtual addresses on to the real store poses a number of problems not encountered with the segmented systems. The number of pages in each process virtual store is usually quite large. For example, page sizes typically vary between 0.5 Kbyte and 4 Kbytes, so that on a machine with a 32-bit virtual address, each process might have between one and eight million pages. Although it may be possible to apply certain restrictions on the user so that a much more limited virtual addressing space is used, the number of pages required by a process is still quite large.

The mapping of a large number of pages precludes the use of base registers such as those described in chapter 5 for segmented machines. To avoid the high cost of these registers, a logically equivalent technique would be to have a page table for each process resident in memory, as illustrated in figure 6.2. This is indexed by the page field of the virtual address to yield the corresponding real page number.

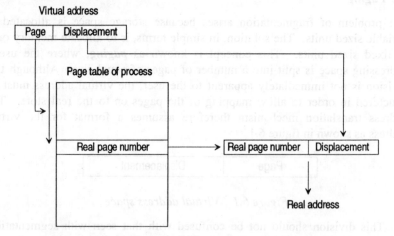

Figure 6.2   Direct mapping of virtual address in a paged machine

The main disadvantage with this technique, apart from the very large size of the page table, is that every location accessed would require an additional memory access in order to translate the virtual address. Clearly, suitable caching of the page table entries would be required to avoid a significant degradation in the overall system performance.

6.2 Paged segmented machines

One of the disadvantages with the paged systems described so far is the large page table that has to be maintained for each process. This was avoided in early implementations of paging by providing a complete mapping of the real memory using associative *page address registers,* where each physical page had a register containing the corresponding virtual address. This is clearly inflexible and excessive with large memories, so alternative schemes were developed using *current page registers.* These are also associative but fewer in number, and perform the translation between a subset of the virtual pages and corresponding real page numbers. The registers are loaded by the address translation hardware from the system tables whenever access is made to a page not held within the current page registers. This requires that the system tables are organised in a suitable form for easy and efficient access by the hardware.

A very effective solution is clearly illustrated on machines that combine the techniques of both paging and segmentation. The intention of these machines is to enjoy the benefits of a segmented virtual store, as with the multiple base-limit register machines, while using paging to eliminate the problems of external fragmentation (Daley and Dennis, 1968; Buckle, 1978; Kilburn *et al.,* 1968). The virtual addressing space on these machines is divided into fields as shown in figure 6.3.

Segment	Page	Displacement

Figure 6.3   Paged segmented addressing

In this case there are three fields in each address giving:

(a) segment
(b) page within a segment
(c) displacement within a page

The retrieval of the real address of a page is therefore achieved by successively indexing into a segment table and page table, as shown in figure 6.4. Although this implies several memory accesses to retrieve the address of a particular page, suitable caching of the virtual and real page addresses can reduce the overheads, given that programs will usually make many accesses to the same set of pages.

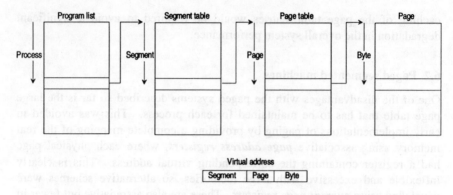

Figure 6.4   Address translation using segment and page tables

The tables used for address translation can be regarded as forming a tree structure with the program list at the top level.

Program list   This has one entry per process and contains a pointer to the segment table for each process.

Segment table   There is one segment table per process, which describes the segments available to a process, and the location of the page table for each of those segments.

Page table   Each segment has a page table, which gives the location of all of the pages within that segment.

Although this structure potentially occupies considerably more table space than the simple linear page table described earlier or a table searched associatively, this system relies on two important factors. Firstly, programs do not access all of the segments available in the virtual store and so page tables will not need to be allocated for undefined segments. Secondly, the page tables can be swapped in and out of memory so that only those for segments currently in use need be resident in memory.

6.2.1 Memory management in a paged segmented machine

The main data structures of the memory management system are the segment and page tables that map the virtual store on to the real memory. To a great extent, the format of these is defined by the address translation hardware of the machine. It is therefore the responsibility of the system architect in specifying the address translation system to ensure that the virtual store has the desired characteristics. A fairly typical organisation is shown in figure 6.5. This is based on the paged segmented structure already outlined, with the additional refinement of allowing process and system segment tables to assist in the sharing of segments. The provision of common segments would also be possible, although it has been omitted in this example for the sake of simplicity.

(a) Segment table base register

The root of the address translation system is the segment table base register. This contains the address of the segment table for the current process, and hence defines the virtual address space currently accessible. This register is reloaded on process changing, with the effect that an entirely new virtual store is brought into use. In addition to the address of the segment table, this register might also contain a limit field giving the size of the process segment table, and hence the maximum segment number accessible by the process. On systems supporting common segments as outlined in chapter 5, a separate but similarly structured register may be loaded at system start time to point to a common segment table.

(b) Process segment table

Each process segment table has three fields which serve the following functions.

(1) Status

This indicates whether the segment has been defined by the user. As all segments have attributes, such as a size and access permission, it is necessary for users to tell the operating system whenever a segment is required and the attributes to be associated with it. The operating system is then able to allocate a system segment table entry and initialise both segment tables appropriately. If a process attempts to access a segment that is not marked as defined, then a program fault condition exists.

(2) Access permission

This is similar to the permission information in the purely segmented system described in chapter 5. Some systems include an additional permission bit to show that the segment is accessible only by the operating system. Other systems cater for several levels of privilege within the machine by allocating several bits for each of the read, write and obey states. This is discussed further in chapter 9.

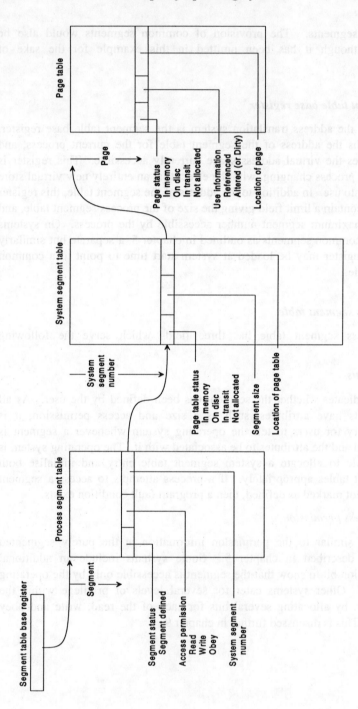

Figure 6.5 Address Translation in a paged segmented system

(3) Location of the system segment table entry

This field allows the address translation system to access the system segment table entry that was allocated when the segment was defined. On some machines, where the system segment table begins at a known address, this field might be replaced by a (more compact) system segment number SSN.

(c) System segment table

The system segment table has three fields, as follows:

(1) Page table status

This indicates the position of the page table. In general, four options are possible: the page table could be in memory, on the disk, in transit between the disk and memory or, if the segment has not previously been accessed, space might not have been allocated for it.

(2) Segment size

This is examined by the address translation hardware to check for accesses beyond the defined size of the segment.

(3) Location of the page table

Depending on the status, this field contains the address of the page table either in memory or on the backing store.

(d) Page table

The page table has a status field and location field similar to those in the segment table, except that they relate to the status of the pages in a segment rather than the page table. The third field contains information about the usage of the page. In general, this will be updated whenever a current page register is loaded for the page. If the attempted access is for reading, the referenced bit will be set. If a write access is attempted, both the referenced and altered bits will be set.

6.3 Algorithms and performance

In chapter 5 and so far in this chapter the development of memory management systems leading to the design of paging systems has been discussed. The performance of paging systems will now be considered.

The performance of a program varies considerably with the number of pages that it has in memory. On entering a process, because there are very few pages in memory, relatively few instructions can be obeyed before there is a virtual store interrupt. If it is possible to have all of a program and its data in memory, then no virtual store interrupts occur. The behaviour of a program can be summarised as shown in figure 6.6.

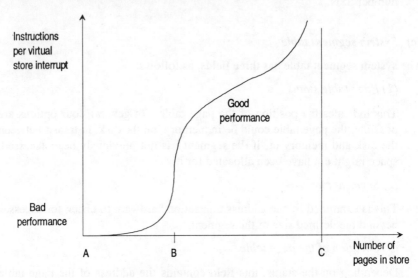

Figure 6.6   Performance of a paging system

Between points A and B, the performance of the machine is extremely poor. However, on approaching point B, the pages most frequently used by the program are in memory and so the performance of the machine improves dramatically. The number of pages for which this happens in known as the *working set*. The working set varies between programs, and between different phases in the execution of a program (for example, editing, compiling, running).

Between points B and C, the performance continues to improve but at a much more gradual rate. At point C, all of the program is in memory and so there are no more virtual store interrupts.

If there are a number of programs in memory together, as might happen in multiprogramming in a time-sharing system, it is difficult to decide how much memory each program should be allowed to occupy. Sufficient space to hold the whole program (point C) could be allocated, but this might be very large indeed. In practice, the performance of the machine will be satisfactory so long as a program has its working set available, and this will generally be considerably less than the total program size.

If a process does not have all of its pages in memory, there will be periods when pages have to be transferred in from the backing store. During this period other processes can be multiprogrammed, so that the central processor is kept busy. The CPU utilisation therefore varies according to the graph in figure 6.7.

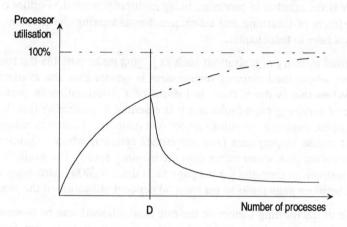

Figure 6.7   CPU utilisation

Up to point D, the utilisation is improving as the level of multi-programming increases. However, when point D is reached, a situation such as the following occurs:

Program 1 requests a page from backing store.

> This triggers store rejection which may decide to reject a page of program 2.

Multiprogramming occurs and program 2 is run.

Program 2 requests a page from backing store.

> This triggers store rejection which decides to reject a page of program 1, etc.

The resulting situation is that no program has its working set in memory and in consequence the performance falls off dramatically. This unstable state is known as *thrashing*, when the performance might drop down to a few per cent (for example, 5 to 10 per cent or less).

To ensure good performance, every process should have its working set in memory, in effect:

$$\sum_{1}^{N} \text{Working sets} \leq \text{Store size}$$

where N is the number of processes being multiprogrammed. Further coverage of the effects of thrashing and techniques for addressing the problem will be described later in this chapter.

Virtual memory organisations such as paging make possible the running of programs whose total memory requirement is greater than the available store size. When this is done, there is inevitably a deterioration in performance because of servicing page faults and it is essential to remember that, beyond a certain point, paging is no substitute for real memory. Failure to acknowledge this fact results in programs (and sometimes systems) whose execution speed depends on the disk speed rather than the memory speed. For example, with a 100 ns instruction time and a 5 ms page fault time, 50,000 instructions must be obeyed between page faults to get even 50 per cent utilisation of the processor.

One of the limiting factors on the rate at which work can be processed in a time-sharing system is the time taken to swap processes to and from main memory. Consider a typical interactive editing activity. The swap time might be the time taken to page in, say, eight 1 Kbyte pages, or

8 × (average latency + page transfer time)

Using the disk performance figures of chapter 5, if the average latency is 8.3 ms, and the page transfer time is 0.4 ms, this gives a swap time of 70 ms. Had the process been swapped in as a single unit, the time would have been

1 × average latency + 8 × page transfer time

or 11.5 ms. Obviously this extension of swap times by a factor of 6 or more is not acceptable.

If the page size is increased, then clearly more information is fetched to memory for each transfer (and hence for each latency time). Thus, provided that the extra data fetched is actually useful, performance can be improved in this way. On the other hand if the extra information turns out not to be required, then time has been wasted in fetching it to memory and (more importantly) it has occupied more memory than necessary. So, for example, fetching eight 1 Kbyte pages would take:

8 × (average latency + page transfer time) = 70 ms

while fetching four 2 Kbyte pages would take

4 × (average latency + 2 page transfer time) = 36.4 ms

Inherent in a paging system is the need for a page table that is available for access. This produces an additional overhead requirement not needed in an unpaged system.

Obviously, if the page size is increased, then the overhead increases, but on the other hand the number of pages per segment (and hence page table size) decreases. Thus a compromise must be made to produce a page size that gives reasonably optimal utilisation.

An alternative consideration would be to have a store hierarchy of more than the two levels so far assumed. For example, there might be several main memories and backing stores, differing in capacity and speed, and different page sizes might be chosen for each of the different levels. Clearly many configurations are possible within such a system, but consider the following case with three levels of store:

(1) Disk
(2) Mass RAM (large but slow)
(3) Small RAM (fast but very limited capacity).

It is advantageous to transfer larger pages between the disk and the mass store than between the mass and small RAMs. If a mass page size of 4 Kbytes and a small page size of 1 Kbyte are used, then the time to fetch four consecutive 1 Kbyte pages from disk to small memory is:

(1 × disk → mass transfer) + (4 × mass → small RAM transfer)

= (1 × average latency + 4 Kbyte transfer time)

+ (4 × 1 Kbyte transfer time)

= (8.3 + 1.6) + (4 × 0.4) = 11.5 ms

On the other hand, if we transferred directly from disk to small RAM in 1 Kbyte pages the time would be:

4 × (average latency + page transfer time) = 34.8 ms

So, by using a different page size at the two levels, transfer times can be improved by a factor of 34.8/11.5. This is clearly the optimal case for these page sizes, as all the pages transferred to mass store are eventually used. In the worst case, only one of the four pages is actually used, so the time would be:

(1 × disk → mass transfer) + (1 × mass → small transfer)

= (1 × average latency + 4 Kbyte transfer time)

+ (1 × 1 Kbyte transfer time)

$$= (8.3 + 1.6) + (1 \times 0.4) = 10.3 \text{ ms}$$

whereas, with direct 1 Kbyte transfers from disk to small memory:

$(1 \times \text{disk} \rightarrow \text{small transfer})$
$= (\text{average latency} + 1 \text{ Kbyte transfer}) = 8.7 \text{ ms}$

Hence, in the worst case the performance decreases by a factor of 10.3/8.7 as a result of using two page sizes. Note, though, that the extra space wasted is in mass rather than the small memory.

The fact that reasonable performance can be achieved with programs greater than memory size is due to the phenomenon, defined in chapter 5, known as *locality*. This can be described informally as a tendency by programs to cluster their page references, and leads to the typical curve for the total number of page faults for a given memory size allocated to a process as shown in figure 6.8.

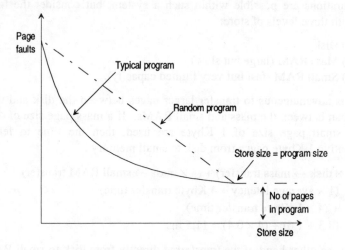

Figure 6.8   Page faults against memory size

Clearly, even for a very large memory, there will be a certain minimum number of page faults to get the pages into memory initially. Once the pages are all in memory the program runs with no further page faults. For memory sizes less than the program size, more page faults may occur as a result of rejecting a page that is subsequently needed again. However, the number of page faults does not increase linearly with decreasing memory size, as some pages that are rejected may never be used again. This is a consequence of locality. A program accessing its pages randomly would tend to give a much worse performance (more page faults) for a given memory size than typical real programs, as illustrated by figure 6.8.

In a time-sharing system, similar remarks can be made about each interaction. At the start of its time slice, a process will tend to have all its pages on backing store and will therefore need to fetch to memory the pages used in the time slice. The number of extra page faults then depends on the amount of memory available to it, which might be the real memory size or the amount of space allocated to it by the operating system.

In principle, locality can be treated as two separate interacting phenomena - *temporal* and *spatial* locality. Temporal locality refers to the high probability of a page that has just been accessed being accessed again soon. Spatial locality refers to the high probability that, if a page is accessed, the adjacent pages will be accessed soon. Both phenomena tend to arise naturally as a result of normal programming practice, and programmers can often greatly improve the performance of their programs by packing procedures or data that are used at the same time physically close together in the store.

From the point of view of the operating system, temporal and spatial locality are not particularly useful concepts, and locality is normally treated as a single phenomenon formalised in the *working set* concept. The working set of a program at a given instant is the set of pages it needs in memory at that instant:

$WS(t,\tau) = \{$pages accessed in the interval $[t, t + \tau]\}$

In practice this set is not usually known by the operating system, but as a result of locality it is very well approximated for small time intervals by

$WS(t,\tau) = \{$pages accessed in the interval $[t - \tau, t]\}$

Often only the *number* of pages required is of interest (so that a sensible amount of space can be allocated) and so the working set size is defined as:

$WSS(t,\tau) = $ number of pages in $WS(t,\tau)$

Intuitively, the working set is the number of pages needed by a process to run reasonably efficiently, so values of τ must be such that a few page requests can be afforded. For example, values of $\tau \geq 50{,}000$ instructions might be reasonable. For a batch process, the working set might typically be around half the total process size; for an interactive process, the total number of pages accessed during a (short) time slice is a good estimate.

6.4 Page replacement algorithms

When a program is run in a small memory, its performance will depend to some extent on the algorithm used to reject pages from memory, that is, the replacement algorithm. Once again it is necessary to stress that, if the memory is excessively small, even the best replacement algorithm cannot give good performance. For reasonable performance, the memory size must be at least as big as the program's working set size. The objective of the replacement algorithm is then to choose a page to replace that which is not in the program's working set. (Note that, for the time being, only a system running a single process is being considered. The effects of multiprogramming will be considered later.)

Three page replacement algorithms will now be considered;

(1) Least recently used (LRU)
(2) First in first out (FIFO)
(3) Not recently used (NRU)

6.4.1 *Least-recently-used algorithm (LRU)*

The phenomenon of program locality means that a program's working set varies slowly with time. Thus the immediate past reference history usually serves as a good predictor for the immediate future, and an excellent algorithm is:

'replace the page which has been used least recently'

That is, the page that has been out of use the longest. This is the least recently used algorithm, and in practice it has been shown to perform well.

The problem with LRU is that it is still difficult to implement; a true LRU implementation requires that the hardware maintain an indication of 'time since last use' for each store page. Without such hardware assistance, the choice of algorithm is effectively limited (for efficiency reasons) to those that use information obtained at page fault times - that is, it is impractical to place a software overhead on every page access, and therefore information can be gathered only during the infrequent (it is hoped) page faults.

The worst case for LRU rejection (and indeed for all 'sensible' non-lookahead algorithms) is a program that accesses its pages cyclically in a memory that is just not large enough. For example, the trace of memory accesses

{0, 1024, 2048, 3072, 4096, 0, 1024, 2048. . . .}

in a 4 Kbyte memory with 1 Kbyte page size gives a page fault for every reference. The optimal choice for rejection in this case is always the *most recently accessed* page, which is contrary to expectations from the locality principle. (Obviously, programs with cyclic access patterns exhibit very poor temporal locality.)

6.4.2 First-in-first-out algorithm (FIFO)

The FIFO algorithm is quite commonly used as it is very easy to implement. It consists in replacing the page that has been in memory the longest. It is not difficult to find intuitive justifications for the choice - a page fetched to memory a long time ago may now have fallen out of use. On the other hand it might have been in constant use since it was fetched, in which case it would be a poor replacement choice.

FIFO replacement again performs very badly with cyclic accessing. However, it also exhibits another kind of bad behaviour, known as the FIFO anomaly. For certain page traces, it is possible with FIFO replacement that the number of page faults increases when the memory size is increased. Obviously this is a highly undesirable situation. Although an increase in the real memory size of a machine is a relatively rare event, the FIFO anomaly could be serious in a paged multiprogramming system. Here the operating system might allocate a 'quota' of memory to each process, increasing the size of a process's quota if it suffers too many page faults. The effect of the FIFO anomaly is potentially disastrous.

As an example of the anomaly, consider the page trace

{4, 3, 2, 1, 4, 3, 5, 4, 3, 2, 1, 5}

running in memory of sizes 3 and 4 pages. With a memory of size 3 pages, there are 9 page faults, as indicated by '*':

{4*, 3*, 2*, 1*, 4*, 3*, 5*, 4, 3, 2*, 1*, 5}

If the memory size is increased to 4 pages, there are 10 page faults:

{4*, 3*, 2*, 1*, 4, 3, 5*, 4*, 3*, 2*, 1*, 5*}

Note that rejection is based on the longest time in memory without regard to most recent access.

For comparison, the corresponding cases using LRU would give:

For 3 pages of memory, there are 10 page faults

{4*, 3*, 2*, 1*, 4*, 3*, 5*, 4, 3, 2*, 1*, 5*}

For 4 pages of memory, there are 8 page faults

{4*, 3*, 2*, 1*, 4, 3, 5*, 4, 3, 2*, 1*, 5*}

The existence of such pathological cases gives some cause for worry about the use of algorithms such as FIFO. It will be shown that LRU, and a whole class of algorithms called *stack algorithms* to which it belongs, do not exhibit this behaviour. Before doing this, however, we will look at one more commonly used replacement algorithm.

6.4.3 Not-recently-used algorithm (NRU)

The NRU algorithm tries to partition the pages in memory into two groups: those that have been used 'recently', and those that have not. It then rejects any page that has not been used recently. The most common implementation consists of a FIFO replacement algorithm, modified to give recently used pages a second chance. It operates as follows:

> Whenever a page is accessed, it is marked as 'referenced'. (This requires hardware support, but is fairly inexpensively achieved, and is included in most paging hardware.) When it is required to reject a page, a cyclic scan of the pages in memory is made (as in the FIFO algorithm). If the page being considered is not marked as 'referenced', it is rejected as usual. If it marked as 'referenced', it is altered to 'not referenced', and the reject algorithm moves on to consider the next page. Next time this page is considered it will be marked 'not referenced' unless it has been accessed again in the meantime.

Obviously this algorithm is easy to implement - almost as easy as the simple FIFO algorithm - and gives an approximation to the LRU algorithm. Consequently, it tends to give better performance than the straightforward FIFO. However, it does still suffer from the FIFO anomaly for some page traces (not necessarily the same page traces as for FIFO though).

The NRU idea can be generalised to give a closer approximation to LRU by partitioning into more than two groups and rejecting from the 'least recently used' group. The easiest way to do this is to associate a counter with each page. Whenever the page is referenced, the counter is set to some value x. Each time a page is considered for rejection, its counter is decremented and the page is rejected only when the counter falls to zero. Obviously, the value of x needs careful tuning since if it is too high, many redundant passes will be made through the list of pages before finally choosing a suitable candidate to reject. It is possible over a period of time to adjust x to obtain the optimum spread of pages into groups such that there are always pages available in the 'zero' (replaceable) group.

6.4.4 Stack algorithms

Although it may not arise frequently, the FIFO anomaly is somewhat worrying in the context of multiprogramming systems, where it can defeat attempts to calculate optimal memory allocations for processes. There is therefore interest in defining algorithms that do not exhibit anomalous behaviour. A class of algorithms known as *stack algorithms,* of which LRU is a member, can be shown not to suffer from the FIFO anomaly. A stack algorithm is defined as follows:

> Let $S(A, P, k, N)$ be the set of pages in memory when processing reference k of the page trace P using replacement algorithm A in a memory of size N pages.

> Then A is a stack algorithm if, for all P, k, and N:

> $$S(A, P, k, N) \subseteq S(A, P, k, N + 1)$$

That is, if the memory size is increased, then at any instant in time the same set of pages are in memory as for the smaller size, plus possibly some more. Obviously if this is satisfied it is not possible to suffer more page faults with the larger memory size.

> It is very easy to show that LRU is a stack algorithm. For

> $S(LRU, P, k, N)$ = the last N distinct pages referenced in P
> $S(LRU, P, k, N + 1)$ = the last $N + 1$ distinct pages referenced in P

and quite clearly, $S(LRU, P, k, N) \subseteq S(LRU, P, k, N + 1)$.

6.5 Multiprogramming

So far only the effects of paging for a single user have been considered. However, a system capable of supporting multiprogramming is required and the existence of such a requirement imposes new criteria on the paging system. It has already been noted that the time taken to 'swap-in' a process in a demand paging system (that is, to fetch its working set to memory) can be much greater than the time for a process of equivalent size in an unpaged system because latency costs are incurred on each page transfer rather than just once for the entire process.

The effect of this extended swap time is to increase the 'effective' service times of processes. In a system where swapping and computing are partially overlapped, the effective service time is max(q, s) where q is the average CPU time used per time slice and s is the swap time. Thus a large increase in s tends to make $s \gg q$, and so the response time for a given number of users increases drastically. (Conversely, the number of users who can be serviced with a given response time falls.)

Clearly, the factor that limits response times is 'number of processes swapped per second', rather than the swap time for individual processes, though the two are related. This means that one of two main strategies can be adopted to improve performance:

(1) Reduce the time taken to swap individual processes.
(2) Improve the swap rates by swapping in more than one process at once.

To reduce individual process swap times, the latency that occurs between page transfers must somehow be eliminated or at least reduced. One approach might be to try to place the pages of a process on the backing store in such a way that these latencies were minimised. This is very difficult since it is not usually possible to predict the precise sequence and timing of page transfers, and hence to know where pages are to be placed. (However, with moving-head devices (disks) it certainly *does* pay to try to keep all the pages of a process together, so as to minimise seek times.)

The difficulty mentioned above is a result of using demand paging, so the process itself determines the order in which pages are requested and the timing of the requests. A more effective strategy is therefore to try to prefetch a process's pages without waiting for them to be demanded. In general this is not possible; but at the start of the time slice it is known that a process will have to fetch its working set to memory. Furthermore, a reasonable estimate can be made about which pages are in the working set, by noting which ones were accessed during the previous time slice. If, before running a process, the system arranges to prefetch its working set to memory, the order in which the pages are to be fetched can be determined so as to reduce latencies. This may or may not be coupled with judicious placement of pages on the backing store but, even without this, a better performance would be expected just from scheduling transfers in the optimum sequence.

The disadvantage of prepaging is, of course, that it can result in many redundant page transfers when a process changes its working set. This happens for example if a user switches to a new kind of activity or even if the process switches to a new phase. So, there is some attraction in devising efficient policies that still make use of demand paging.

As already observed, the requirement is for the operating system to have some control over the order in which page transfers are serviced. This is not possible for a single process under demand paging. However, with many processes, if each has a page request outstanding, choice can be made to service these in a sequence that minimises latencies. (In practice, of course, the page requests are serviced as they occur and transfer requests are passed on to the disk manager. It is the disk manager that maintains a queue of outstanding transfer requests and chooses which to service next.)

The following is one way of organising such a system. The coordinator maintains a list of processes in the current 'multiprogramming mix' (which may be a subset of all the processes in the system) in priority order. Whenever the highest priority process is halted, the next is entered, and so on. Whenever any process completes its time slice it is moved to the end of the list, and all the processes beneath it move up one place.

The effect of this strategy is as follows. It is hoped that, by the time a process reaches the top priority position, its working set is in memory. Whenever it suffers a page fault (infrequently) the next process is entered, and so on. Between them, the top few processes are able to use most of the processor time. Whenever one of the processes lower down the queue is entered, it is likely to suffer an immediate page fault as it has not yet established its working set in memory. This causes the next process to be entered, make an immediate page request, and so on. The overall effect is that a number of page requests are generated in very rapid succession and the system can then service these in an optimum sequence. Thus several processes are being swapped simultaneously. The effect on performance is similar to prepaging, but only pages that are actually required are fetched.

The scheme has two main disadvantages as compared with prepaging. The first is that a larger quantity of memory is needed. For a prepaging system, only enough space for two processes is needed: one running and the other being prepaged. If multiprogramming several processes, then enough storage space for all of them must be available. The second disadvantage applies only to systems that use a moving-head device as a backing store. Since pages are being fetched for several different processes at once, there is a much higher probability that successive page requests will be on different tracks and thus will incur seek overheads as well as rotational latency.

6.5.1 Thrashing

When several processes are multiprogrammed in a paging system, it was shown that a phenomenon known as thrashing can occur. Thrashing is an instability that arises when the total memory requirements of the processes being multiprogrammed exceeds the available main memory size. As an example, consider two processes A and B, accessing 4 pages each in a memory of size 7 pages. A possible sequence of events is as follows:

A accesses page A1;	page fault;	A halted
B accesses page B1;	page fault;	B halted
A accesses page A2;	page fault;	A halted
B accesses page B2;	page fault;	B halted
A accesses page A3;	page fault;	A halted
B accesses page B3;	page fault;	B halted
A accesses page A4;	page fault;	A halted
B accesses page B4;	page fault;	
	A1 rejected;	B halted
A accesses page A1;	page fault;	
	B1 rejected;	A halted
B accesses page B1;	page fault;	
	A2 rejected;	B halted

The overall effect is that almost no useful instructions are executed. Either process would run alone with almost 100 per cent efficiency; when they are multiprogrammed in the above way, efficiency drops to only a few per cent. This is a very serious problem that has been observed on most paged computing systems. Obviously, the above is an extreme example but it can be said with certainty that if the sum of the working sets of all processes being multiprogrammed exceeds the available memory size, performance will deteriorate to an unacceptable level.

Thrashing is due to interference between processes being multi-programmed; that is, each process is continually causing rejection of a page in the working set of one of the others. Two possible strategies to prevent the thrashing are:

(i) by load control - Limit multiprogramming to a 'safe' level - that is, such that the sum of the working sets is less than the memory size.

(ii) by controlling interference - Prevent interference between processes being multiprogrammed.

In the case of prevention by load control the level of multiprogramming is limited so that all active working sets fit into memory. This applies only to the very rapid multiprogramming that arises for events like page transfers. Many more processes can still be dealt with by multiprogramming on longer-term events such as terminal input/output. Effectively, the coordinator must restrict itself (or be restricted) to a subset; other schedulers such as the process scheduler can still deal with all processes. The total number of processes in the system is still determined by response time considerations.

Three main forms of load control can be identified for the prevention of thrashing:

(1) Fixed safe multiprogramming level.
(2) Multiprogramming level based on working set estimates.
(3) Multiprogramming level adjusted iteratively, depending on page fault frequency.

The first obviously suffers from an inability to deal with extreme processes: smaller than average processes cause space to be wasted, larger than average ones may cause thrashing to occur. This can be offset to some extent in a batch system by giving the operator control over the multiprogramming level, although it is not always easy or convenient for the operator to react quickly to changes in the loading.

If the system can make an estimate of a process's working set size by monitoring its page references, then these estimates can be used to control multiprogramming, by considering only processes such that the sum of their working sets fit into memory. In a time-sharing system, a suitable estimate may be the number of pages referenced in the previous time slice. This method operates well in conjunction with the prepaging strategies discussed earlier.

Finally it is possible to adjust the level of multiprogramming automatically, effectively by trying to detect thrashing when it begins to occur. This is done by monitoring the frequency of page faults: if they occur too often the multiprogramming level is reduced, if they occur with less than a certain threshold frequency it is increased. The main problem here is that individual processes with very bad paging characteristics can have a disastrous effect on the multiprogramming level.

The interference that causes thrashing is brought about when one process causes pages in the working set of another to be rejected from memory. This form of interference can be prevented by controlling the extent to which processes may reject one another's pages, and forms the basis of the second strategy to prevent thrashing.

Most systems operate by assigning a *quota* of pages (possibly based on working set estimates) to each process, such that all quotas fit into memory. Each process is then allowed to reject pages of others until it has its quota of store pages; after this it may be allowed to take further pages if they are free, but if rejection becomes necessary it is forced to reject one of its own pages. Thus the replacement algorithm is required to operate *locally* within each process rather than globally on all processes in the system. This is clearly a sensible policy since the majority of replacement algorithms are designed to take advantage of the reference properties of individual processes. Obviously there are many variants, depending on exactly *how* the quotas are assigned (by compilers, users, operators or automatically by the system) and what algorithm is used for rejection.

There are also strategies that do not involve explicitly assigning quotas, of which the following is fairly typical. The processes are ordered in the multiprogramming mix according to their relative priorities and an indication is kept with each page of the priority of its owning process. Then, processes are allowed to reject pages of processes at their own and lower-priority levels, but never of higher-priority ones. Clearly this prevents thrashing. However, it does tend to result in an accumulation of little-used pages for the higher-priority processes, and it has been suggested that memory utilisation is improved by choosing a random page at intervals and rejecting it.

It should be noted that these policies are designed to prevent the total collapse of performance as a result of thrashing. Individual processes may still perform very badly if they are too large for the quotas assigned, but at least they do not cause other, well-behaved processes to suffer. Thus overall system utilisation may be quite high even in the presence of one or two badly behaved processes.

6.6 Storage allocation techniques

The allocation of storage also presents a major problem to the designer of memory management systems, and it is also an area in which many different algorithms are currently in use. The choice of a suitable allocation strategy is not just appropriate for the allocation of main memory but also for the allocation of space on the backing store, and in general, a system may use different algorithms for each level in the storage hierarchy.

Inevitably, the choice of algorithm involves a compromise, and in this case the aim is to achieve the most effective utilisation of the store while at the same time performing the allocation efficiently. The 'efficiency' of the technique is assessed in terms of the speed with which an area of store can be allocated and in terms of the space occupied by the data structures needed to monitor the usage of the store. When large backing stores are considered, this latter aspect can be particularly crucial.

In general, the allocation of space on a paged machine is considerably simpler than on a purely segmented machine. As all the pages in memory are of equal size, it is largely irrelevant as to which is allocated whenever a new page is required. The emphasis therefore is on using the fastest technique for performing the allocation, as any page chosen is equally good. As was seen in chapter 5, the situation is not as simple with segmented machines.

Fragmentation can have a significant effect on the utilisation of the memory, and as a consequence, degrade the overall efficiency and throughput of the system.

The choice of data structures for monitoring the usage of the store is largely determined by the characteristics of the storage medium concerned. Two main techniques are used; (a) a linked list, where free blocks are chained together using the first few locations of each block to hold the size and linkage information, and (b) a bit vector, where each bit corresponds to a block of a certain unit size and indicates whether the block is free or allocated. In this case, larger areas than the unit size are allocated by searching for multiple consecutive free blocks. The first technique is really only applicable to the allocation of space in the main memory, as it is impractical to chain together free blocks on a disk.

The most common techniques for performing the allocation of store are known as (a) the first fit algorithm, (b) the next fit algorithm, (c) the best fit algorithm, (d) the worst fit algorithm and (e) a buddy system. Their principles are outlined below, and they are examined in more detail by Knuth (1973). No technique should be regarded as universally the 'best' as each can be effective under different circumstances.

6.6.1 First fit algorithm

With this technique, the list of free blocks (or the bit vector) is scanned until a block of at least the required size is found. The block is allocated with any excess space being returned to the pool of free blocks. Each time a new block is required, the search is started from the beginning of the list. The effect of this is that small blocks are more readily allocated at the start of memory, whereas more of the list has to be scanned if the store is relatively full or if larger areas are required.

6.6.2 Next fit algorithm

This technique, also known as the modified first fit algorithm, operates in a similar way to the first fit technique except that whenever a block is required, the search is started from the point reached the previous time. It is, in effect, a cyclic scan of the list of free blocks. As a consequence, there is a more even distribution in the allocation of storage, normally with lower search times. However, it has a higher potential for failing to allocate a block due to fragmentation.

6.6.3 Best fit algorithm

This technique allocates the block closest to the required size. Inevitably it involves scanning the entire list of free blocks (unless a block of the *exact* size is found before reaching the end). It is therefore quite costly in terms of the time spent searching the data structures, although it produces a good utilisation of the store.

6.6.4 Worst fit algorithm

A criticism of the best fit algorithm is that the space remaining after allocating a block of the required size is so small that in general it is of no real use. The worst fit algorithm therefore allocates space from the block which will leave the largest portion of free space. The hope is that this will be large enough to satisfy another request. It has the disadvantage, however, that the largest blocks are allocated first and so a request for a large area is more likely to fail.

6.6.5 Buddy system

The buddy system operates by allocating space in a limited number of sizes, for example, powers of 2 of the minimum block size. A separate list is kept of the blocks of each size, thus allocating a block merely involves removing a block from the appropriate list. If the list is empty, a block of the next larger size is split in order to satisfy the request, and the excess space is relinked on to the list of the appropriate size. When space is released, the block is linked into the appropriate free list, but if it is found that the adjacent blocks (its buddies) are also free, then these may be combined to form a free block of the next larger size.

This scheme is effective in that allocation of space is fast, but it does not necessarily produce the optimal utilisation of the store due to the restriction of only allocating space in a limited number of sizes.

6.7 Summary

A number of problems in implementing a memory management system were discussed in chapter 5. Segmentation provides an effective solution to some of these, but with segments being of a variable size, the problem of fragmentation still remains. Paging systems resolve this difficulty by providing a mapping of the memory in fixed size units. This chapter describes the design of a paging system, and in particular, discusses how a system using both paging and segmentation could be implemented. Such systems are now very common, although practical implementations often confuse the logical structuring which is derived from segmentation, with the physical mapping issues which are addressed via paging.

Although the memory size of computers is now potentially very large, applications have expanded such that the demand loading and swapping out of pages is still necessary. The concept of a program's working set has been introduced, being the subset of pages which must be resident in RAM for a process to execute with reasonable efficiency and relatively infrequent virtual store interrupts. The effects of multiprogramming on memory utilisation have also been described, and in this context, the problem of thrashing was introduced. Possible solutions through load control and control of interference were presented.

This chapter has also examined a number of algorithms which may be used within memory management systems. The first group are concerned with the choice of page for rejection from memory when space is required. These page replacement algorithms include least-recently-used, first-in-first-out and not-recently-used strategies. The characteristics of these, difficulties in their implementation and anomalies in their behaviour have been discussed.

The second group of algorithms is concerned with the allocation of memory. These algorithms would be suitable for the allocation of space in RAM, blocks on the disk (such as for files), and even within other applications which include the dynamic allocation of space, such as within a compiler. The algorithms include first fit, next fit, best fit, worst fit and buddy systems, and are most applicable to the allocation of space in variable sized units.

6.8 References and bibliography

A.P. Batson, S. Ju and D. Wood (1970). 'Measurements of Segment Size', *Communications of the ACM*, Vol. 13, No. 3, pp. 155-9.

J.K. Buckle (1978). *The ICL2900 Series*, Macmillan, London.

P. Calingaert (1967). 'System Performance Evaluation: Survey and Appraisal', *Communications of the ACM*, Vol. 10, pp. 12-18.

W.W. Chu and H. Opderbeck (1974). 'Performance of Replacement Algorithms with Different Page Sizes', *Computer*, Vol. 7, No. 11, pp. 14-21.

R.C. Daley and J.B. Dennis (1968). 'Virtual Memory, Processes, and Sharing in MULTICS', *Communications of the ACM*, Vol. 11, pp. 306-12.

P.J. Denning (1968). 'The Working Set Model for Program Behavior', *Communications of the ACM*, Vol. 11, No. 5, pp. 323-33.

T. Kilburn, D. Morris, J.S. Rohl and F.H. Sumner (1968). 'A System Design Proposal', *Proceedings of the IFIP Conference*, Edinburgh.

D.E. Knuth (1973). *The Art of Computer Programming, Volume 1 Fundamental Algorithms*, Addison-Wesley, Reading, Mass.

H. Lucas (1971). 'Performance Evaluation and Monitoring', *ACM Computing Surveys*, Vol. 3, pp. 79-91.

W.C. Lynch (1972). 'Operating System Performance', *Communications of the ACM*, Vol. 15, pp. 579-85.

R.L. Mattson, J. Gecsei, D.R. Slutz and I.L. Traiger (1970). 'Evaluation Techniques for Storage Hierarchies', *IBM Systems Journal*, Vol. 9, No. 2, pp. 78-117.

7 File Management

7.1 Requirements of a file system

Most users of a computer utilise the facilities of the file system without being aware of the complexity that lies behind it. In general, this complexity does not result because of the nature of the facilities provided, rather because of the need to ensure the security and integrity of the file system. It is usually this aspect of an operating system's design which has the greatest impact on users, and which also has the greatest visibility when it fails to function as desired.

Before examining this potentially rather complex aspect of system design, the fundamental characteristics of a file system will be examined. In principle, the facilities that are expected of a file system are quite simple. The following would be a fairly typical set:

(1) To be able to create and delete files.

(2) To be able to control access to the files, such as by preventing a data file from being obeyed.

(3) To be able to refer to files by symbolic name, and not to worry about the precise location of the files on the backing store.

(4) To be able to share files.

(5) To be able to list the files currently owned by a user.

(6) To have the files protected against failure of the operating system and/or the hardware.

The system manager might have further requirements, such as:

(7) The ability to introduce new users or delete users and their files from the system.

(8) The ability to introduce new storage media, such as additional disks or magnetic tapes for use by the file system. This is, of course, part of the user functionality for personal computers.

103

In general, the provision of these facilities relies on preserving information about the files on the backing store, and on ensuring the security and integrity of the file system. The following attributes of a file management system are therefore considered in this chapter:

(1) Directories and access rights.
(2) Dumping and archiving.
(3) Security of the file system.

The chapter will also look at the characteristics of one particular file system in some depth, namely that of UNIX.

7.2 Directories and access rights

The provision of the user facilities tends to revolve around providing a suitable *catalogue* or *directory* of files belonging to each user. Each directory entry contains fields to indicate:

(a) The symbolic name of the file.
(b) The size and position of the file on the backing store.
(c) The access permitted to the file.

Most of the general user requirements can be satisfied by allowing a user to add or delete entries and list the contents of the directory (items 1, 3 and 5). The provision of shared files (item 4) is a much more complex topic and depends largely on the relationship between directories and on maintaining permission information with each directory stating how other users may access the files.

In many respects, associating access permission information with each file is of use even for protecting the file from illegal accesses by its *owner*. This permission information is very similar to that described in chapter 5 for segments, as a file may have read, write and obey access permissions. Thus, for example, a text file would have read and write access associated with it, so that when the file is opened it can be edited; a precompiled program would have obey access (or read and obey access) associated with it.

In addition to the permission information that states how a file may be accessed when in use, there may also be permission information stating how the file (or directory entry) may be changed. This is of particular significance for users other than the owner of a file, and may state whether a file can be deleted, updated or perhaps renamed.

The structure of the directories and the relationship between them is the main area where file systems tend to differ, and it is also the area that has the most significant effect on the user interface with the file system. Two directory structures will be described here: (a) a single-level directory, and (b) a hierarchical directory.

7.2.1 Single-level directory structure

In the simplest situation, the system maintains a *master block* that has one entry for each user of the computer. The master block entries contain the address of the individual directories so that, in effect, all directories are at the same level and all users are regarded equally. An example of this type of system is illustrated in figure 7.1.

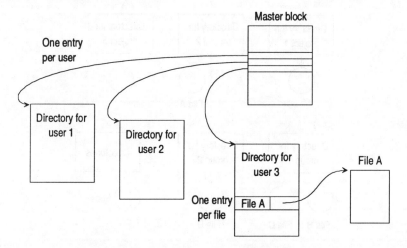

Figure 7.1   Single-level directory structure

When a user logs-on to the computer, the directory (and all the files) associated with that user name are available for use. In order to share files, one needs to indicate the user who owns the file as well as the file name. Additional protection is often provided when sharing files, either by requiring a password to gain access to the file, or by having the owner provide a list of users who can access the file.

This single-level directory may be adequate in the situation where all users are of equal status, such as a class of students in a laboratory. However, in other situations, the environment lends itself to a differential structure of directories which might reflect the nature of the organisation using the computer. One approach to this is provided by the hierarchical directory structure.

7.2.2 *Hierarchical directory structure*

The primary benefit of having a hierarchical directory structure is that it reflects the management structure within organisations, and therefore facilitates the control of users and their resources. There might also be additional benefits for the higher members in the hierarchy when they wish to access the files of their subordinates. Such a scheme is illustrated in figure 7.2.

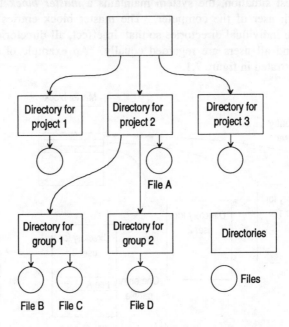

Figure 7.2   Hierarchical directory structure

Here access to files is again made through the appropriate directory; for example, the Group 1 user is able to access the files (File B and File C) under that directory. Access between directories is normally permissible only on a hierarchical basis. Thus, the user Project 2 can gain access to the files under its directory (File A) and to the files in the directories of Group 1 and Group 2. As with the single-level directory structure, restrictions such as password checks may apply if the users Project 1 or Project 3 wish to access these directories or files.

Most systems now support a hierarchical structure for their main file system, as the benefits of allowing a user to organise their files in a structured way are significant, even for single user systems. Further examples of a hierarchical directory structure and how it may be organised are provided in section 7.5, where the UNIX file system is outlined.

7.3 Dumping and archiving

One of the greatest problems in maintaining a file system is to ensure that the information within the files is not corrupted, either by hardware failure or faults in the system software. A guarantee cannot be given that faults will not occur, and so at least a facility must be available to recover files from earlier versions, should they become corrupt.

The normal way of ensuring that additional copies of a file are maintained is by periodically dumping the file store on to some suitable bulk storage media. For example, a disk may be copied every morning on to a back-up disk cartridge. If the disk becomes corrupted during the day, the files as they were at the end of the previous day can be recovered from the back-up disk.

This is quite satisfactory where comparatively small amounts of data are involved but, on a very large system, the time to copy the complete file store is prohibitively long. The alternative therefore is to dump only those files that have been altered since the previous dump was taken - this procedure is referred to as incremental back-up. Although more efficient in terms of the time taken to generate a back-up, it might involve a considerable amount of additional processing to keep track of the latest version of a file across possibly several dump tapes or disks.

Archiving is a facility for deliberately forcing an additional copy of a file to some form of offline media, such as a private disk or tape. This is usually invoked by a user, who wishes either an extra secure version of the file or is wanting some long-term storage of the file outside the normal file system.

In some systems it is possible for the operating system to keep a record of when files are used and to invoke automatic file archiving for those which remain unused for long periods. At the same time the user is notified that the relevant files have been archived. Large systems often use this technique to recover file space held by unused files on the fast storage media. Such a technique means that once the archived version is made the original file in the file system is deleted.

Archived files can be restored back into the file system on explicit request, but as the archive media (such as tapes) may have to be mounted on to a peripheral device, there may be a significant delay before the user can gain access to the file.

7.4 Secure file updating

At the beginning of this chapter it was shown that access permission provided a level of file security by preventing a user from corrupting a file. Corruption can also occur if faults arise in the hardware or system software, and although dumping and archiving can provide a means of recovering a file once it has been corrupted, it is far better if the files are not corrupted in the first place. There are a number of 'tricks' that the software can use to try to prevent faults occurring.

If we consider, as in figure 7.3 for a single-level directory, that the secondary storage contains a master block pointing to directories for each user, which in turn point to the user files, there is a serious problem with the way in which these are updated.

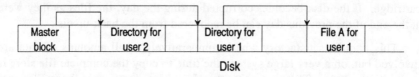

| Master block | | Directory for user 2 | | Directory for user 1 | | File A for user 1 | |

Disk

Figure 7.3   File storage system

If File A for User 1 is being updated by overwriting the appropriate area on the disk, and if the system fails (through hardware or software errors) while the blocks of the file are being written, it is possible that the area of the disk will contain some blocks of the new File A and some of the old version. This is clearly unsatisfactory as the file is now corrupt. The solution is simply to write the new version to a different area of the disk.

Thus, a new version of File A has now been achieved; the subsequent problem is that the associated file directory has to be updated so that it refers to the new version of File A, and the only secure way of achieving this is to produce a new version of the directory. Similarly, a new version of the master block has to be produced. This corresponds to the situation shown in figure 7.4.

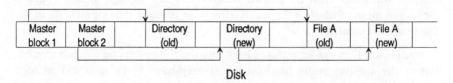

| Master block 1 | Master block 2 | | Directory (old) | | Directory (new) | | File A (old) | | File A (new) | |

Disk

Figure 7.4   File updating system

The question now is: where are the master blocks and how is it possible to distinguish between them? The normal policy is to keep the master blocks at fixed locations on the disk, say at blocks 0 and 1. To distinguish between them, a generation number is kept in the last location of each master block so that when the system is restarted the latest version of the master block (with the last file addition or deletion) is selected. (The last word is used as this should be the very last information transferred to the disk when writing the master blocks.) Checksums may also be included in the master blocks for additional security.

The sequence of writing information to the disk is quite crucial for the updating to be secure. The normal sequence is:

(1) Copy the file to the disk - produce *File A (new)*.
(2) Update directory and copy it to the disk - produce *Directory (new)*.
(3) Update master block and copy it to the alternative position on the disk - produce *Master block 2*.

Having completed such a sequence it is possible to recover all the space occupied by the Directory (old) and File A (old). In some systems, however, once File A (new) is created, File A (old) is preserved as a back-up version of the file. Any subsequent update then makes the file that is updated the new back-up version and automatically deletes the previous back-up version. Such a system is useful during program development since it allows the 'next-most-recent' version to be retained when a file is updated.

In a paged machine, the sequence could be even more complicated, as both the file and the directory could be paged and therefore accessed via a page table. In this case, the sequence adopted could be:

(1) Copy file pages to the disk.
(2) Copy file page table to the disk.
(3) Copy directory pages to the disk.
(4) Copy directory page table to the disk.
(5) Copy the master block to the disk.

7.5 File system of UNIX

The file system structure of UNIX is ostensibly hierarchical, with the system *root* directory being the origin from which all other files or directories may be reached. The file directories normally take the form of a series of directed graphs, thus appearing to the users as a tree structure with files and sub-directories in a hierarchical organisation.

A significant way in which UNIX differs from most other file systems is that management of information specific to a file, such as its size and position, is held separately from the information needed to gain access to the file. Thus the naming conventions implicit in the directory structure, and consequently the checking imposed to gain access to a file, is separate from the physical management of the data in the file. There are strong pragmatic reasons for separating these functions from a file system implementation point of view. However, the separation may be exploited by allowing links to be established between directories to the same file data. A user may therefore access a particular file through multiple pathways. The file system therefore has the potential for being a net structure rather than a strict tree structure.

A UNIX directory contains the file name and a pointer to the file, called the file *i*-number. The *i*-number identifies the *i*-node for the file, and it is the *i*-node which contains the detailed information about the file itself. This includes details of the owner's identification (both user id and group id), protection status, disk block addresses for where the file is stored, file size, time of creation, time of last use, time of last modification, the number of links to the file, and identification as to whether the file is an ordinary file, a special file, or indeed a directory. *I*-nodes themselves are stored in *i*-lists, and the displacement, or offset, of the *i*-node from the start of the *i*-list is the *i*-node's *i*-number.

In UNIX, filenames are constructed by specifying a sequence of directory names separated by slashes '/' and which lead to a particular leaf of a tree. Conventions identify at which point in the tree structure the traversal for a particular pathname should begin. If the pathname begins with a slash, then the path originates at the root directory. Filenames without a leading slash imply that they originate from the current directory, and filenames which start with '../' imply that the path begins with the directory that is the parent of the current directory.

Filenames may also have an extension as a suffix to indicate the nature of the file, such as '.txt' for a text file and '.c' for C source code. Such extensions are not inherent to the file system and are not critical to its operation; they are more of use to application software in checking the nature of the file.

An example of a pathname to a particular file might be:

/usr/fred/letters/april1.txt

where *april1.txt* is an ordinary file which is subordinate to the directory *letters*, which is itself subordinate to the directory *fred* and which is subordinate to *usr*. Finally *usr* is subordinate to the root directory, as specified by the initial '/'. Traversal of the directory structure to arrive at the file *april1.txt* naturally takes place in the reverse order, starting at the root directory.

This form of file addressing represents an absolute pathname to a file. The approach can often be tedious and the alternative is to use a relative pathname, particularly when a user is using several files within a single directory. A user may therefore select a current or working directory as the root for pathname traversals, and in this case the initial '/' is omitted from the pathname. For example, if the current directory is */usr/fred/letters* then the file may be specified simply as *aprill.txt*; if */usr/fred* is current, then the file is specified as *letters/aprill.txt*.

The file itself consists of randomly addressable bytes and its size is the total number of bytes up to a maximum of about 10^9. The file has no structure other than that imposed on it by the user or application software, and hence they use less space than files of fixed-length records, where space is used by unfilled blanks, or files of variable-length records, when there is a count of the number of bytes associated with each record.

The data structures used for managing the file system on UNIX are different from those described in section 7.4, largely due to the introduction of the *i*-nodes and the management of directories as a 'peculiar' type of file. A superblock holds information about the file system as a whole; the *i*-list is the array of *i*-nodes that define the files within the file system; and the remainder of the disk is assigned to file store being either file data blocks or free blocks. All file storage allocation is made in blocks of a fixed size. The disk area on which the files reside is therefore divided into areas as shown in figure 7.5, namely:

(1) Block 0 - usually contains bootstrap.
(2) Block 1 - superblock, contains information such as size of file
         system, the number of *i*-nodes, and free space parameters.
(3) *i*-list which contains one *i*-node for each file.
(4) Blocks used to store files.

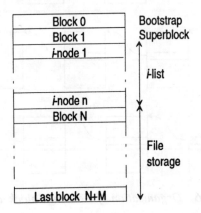

Figure 7.5   Physical disk layout under UNIX

An *i*-node contains the block addresses that are used to access a file, along with other housekeeping information. It therefore holds the following:

(1) Owner's user identification
(2) Owner's group identification
(3) Protection bits
(4) Physical disk addresses for the file data blocks
(5) File size
(6) Time at which the file was created
(7) Time at which the file was last used
(8) Time at which the file was last modified
(9) Time at which the *i*-node was last modified
(10) The number of links to the file
(11) An indication of the nature of the file, for example, whether it is a directory, an ordinary file or a special file.

There are 13 block addresses stored in each *i*-node which are used to gain access to the file data blocks. These are illustrated in figure 7.6.

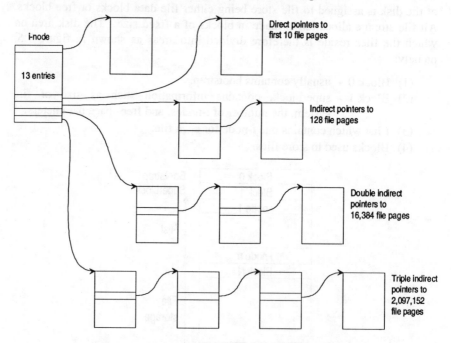

Figure 7.6   Organisation of the i-node block addresses

The disk block size is typically 512 bytes, and for the first 10 blocks of the file, the corresponding block addresses are stored in the first 10 block address locations of the *i*-node. Files which are up to 5120 bytes in size may therefore be accessed directly using these addresses, which makes for very rapid file access, i.e. no further page tables etc. are involved.

For files larger than this, the eleventh address is the address of a block that contains the addresses of the next 128 blocks. This is referred to as an indirect block and allows files of up to 70,656 bytes to be addressed.

A similar principle applies to the twelfth block to give a double indirect block which contains the addresses of a further 128 blocks. Each of these blocks contains the addresses of 128 blocks used to store the file, and hence the double level of indirection. This allows files of up to 8,459,264 bytes ($10 + 128 + 128^2$ blocks of 512 bytes each) to be addressed.

The principle is extended for the thirteenth block to provide a third level of indirection. This allows files of up to 1,082,201,087 bytes ($10 + 128 + 128^2 + 128^3$ blocks of 512 bytes each) to be addressed - the additional last byte can be used to address the next disk drive.

On some configurations, a block size of 1Kbyte is used. This has an immediate effect in that the first 10240 bytes of a file are directly accessible from an *i*-node. It also has further repercussions in that the blocks containing indirect pointers are also doubled in size, thus resulting in a significant expansion in the file size accessible at each level, and allowing files up to 17,247,250,431 bytes ($10 + 256 + 256^2 + 256^3$ blocks of 1024 bytes each).

It is also necessary to have information about the location of free blocks. This information is stored in a linked list of blocks in which a free block contains the pointer to the next free block. In addition to this, the superblock contains the addresses of up to 50 additional free blocks.

It is allowable to read, write or execute a file. In order to provide file protection, a user identification number and a set of 9 protection bits are used. These implement read, write and execute access for the following:

the owner of the file
other members of the owner's group
all other users

For example, listing the protection information for a file might yield the following:

- rwx r-x ---

which shows that the owner is allowed to read, write and execute the file, any member of the owner's group may read and execute only, and no access is permitted for other users. The tenth field (always shown at the start) is used to indicate the type of file, such as a simple file or a directory. In this example, it indicates a simple file (program, data etc.).

7.6 Summary

This chapter has examined the overall requirements of file systems and has discussed various aspects of their implementation, including single level and hierarchical directory structures. The integrity of data within a file system is paramount and so techniques for ensuring that data is not lost have been reviewed. These include dumping and archiving mechanisms and also techniques for ensuring that data is not lost through corruption in the case of system failure.

The chapter concludes with a detailed examination of the UNIX file system, being one of the most distinguishing features of that particular operating system. Implementation details, including the *i*-node organisation and management of the file data blocks have been included.

7.7 References and bibliography

D.E. Denning and P.J. Denning (1979). 'Data Security', *ACM Computing Surveys,* Vol. 11, pp. 227-49.

E.I. Organick (1972). *The Multics System: An Examination of its Structure,* MIT Press, Cambridge, Mass.

8 Resource Management - Deadlocks

8.1 Allocation of resources

One of the major functions of an operating system is to control the resources within the computer system. Indeed, if CPU time and store are regarded as resources, then undoubtedly it is *the* most important function. At a slightly more mundane level, processes need to drive peripherals such as magnetic tape decks or exchangeable disk drives, as users want to mount their own media and have close and dedicated control of the peripherals. In this chapter, the problems of allocating resources to the processes in a multiprogramming system will be examined. As with the allocation of processor time and store, there is a dual objective:

(1) To implement particular management policies with respect to which users get the 'best' service.

(2) To optimise the performance of the system.

The first of these is somewhat outside the scope of this book and so only the second objective will be discussed.

Resource allocation is essentially a scheduling problem: whenever a process requests a resource, a decision must be made on whether to allocate it immediately or to make the process wait. The progress of a process from its creation to its termination can thus be regarded as a number of phases, where the process takes control of some resources and subsequently relinquishes control, as illustrated in figure 8.1.

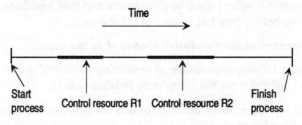

Figure 8.1   Progress of a process during execution

115

This hypothetical system might be one in which input and output devices are under the direct control of user processes and the resources, R1 and R2, might be peripherals. The major problems with resource allocation arise when several processes are concurrently requesting control of the same resources. For simplicity, consider just two processes, P1 and P2.

A resource R1 is assumed to be required by both processes at the same time. Clearly this is not possible, as it is assumed that the resources are such that a single process needs exclusive access to a resource. (Imagine a situation where two processes are simultaneously trying to drive a printer.) The first process to request control of the resource is therefore granted control until it is subsequently released. If the second process requests control during this period, it will be halted until the resource becomes available.

The main problem arises when there are two resources, R1 and R2, available. Consider the following sequence:

P1	P2
Obtain (R2)	Obtain (R1)
Obtain (R1)	
halt waiting for	
P2 to release R1	
	Obtain (R2)
	and halt waiting
	for P1 to release R2

This is a situation known as a *deadlock*, when neither process can run because each is waiting for a resource under the control of the other process.

8.2 Deadlocks

There are five conditions or criteria that, when satisfied, indicate the occurrence of a deadlock.

(1) The processes involved must be *irreversible* and thus unable to reset to an earlier time before they had control of the resources.

(2) Each process must have *exclusive control* of its resources.

(3) There must be *non-preemption* of resources, so that a resource is never released until a process has completely finished with it.

(4) *Resource waiting* must be allowed, so that one process can hold a resource while waiting for another.

(5) There must be a *circular chain* of processes, with each holding resources requested by the next in the chain.

The operating system needs to take explicit action to deal with possible deadlocks. Policies for dealing with deadlocks can broadly be classified as:

(1) Prevention - deadlocks cannot occur because restrictions have been placed on the use of resources.

(2) Detection - deadlocks are detected after they have arisen and action is taken to rectify the problem.

(3) Avoidance - a 'safe' allocation policy is employed and so deadlocks are anticipated and avoided.

8.2.1 Deadlock prevention

Deadlocks may be prevented by placing restrictions on the use of resources such that one or more of the necessary conditions for a deadlock cannot occur. The necessary conditions are:

(1) The resources concerned cannot be shared. This might be achieved by denying the user access to the real, unshareable resources and providing instead a set of 'virtual' resources - for example, spooling achieves this for devices such as printers. However, this cannot be done satisfactorily in all cases - for example, with devices such as magnetic tape and disk drives, the volume of data transferred precludes any attempt at large-scale buffering.

(2) The resources cannot be preempted from the processes holding them. If preemption is possible, then the resources could be reallocated and hence the deadlock resolved, but there are obvious examples where preemption would not be acceptable (for example, a file that has already been half updated to a disk).

(3) Processes hold the resources already allocated while waiting for new ones. One way to avoid this is to allocate all resources at the beginning of a job so that a process does not hold any resources while it is waiting. This is often a reasonable strategy, though it is wasteful for jobs that require certain resources only for short periods of time, and even more so if some resources may not be needed at all (for example, a printer used only to print an error report if the job goes wrong). A variation that partly gets around this is to allow a job to *release* all its resources, then make a fresh request.

(4) A circular chain of processes exists, each process holding a resource required by the next in the chain. This can be avoided by numbering the various resources types and introducing the rule that a process that holds resource k can request only resources numbered $\geq k$. Obviously the disadvantages are the same as mentioned in (3) above, but a suitable numbering of resource types, with commonly used resources given low numbers, can greatly reduce the wastage of resources.

The main resources for which none of the above methods is particularly appropriate are files. Read-only files are clearly shareable, but if files are being altered then, except in specialised situations, the above strategies cannot be used.

8.2.2 Deadlock detection

If none of the above methods of deadlock prevention is suitable, then an attempt could be made to *detect* deadlocks when they occur, and resolve the conflict in some way. Deadlock detection operates by detecting the 'circular wait' condition described in (4) above, and so any algorithm for detecting cycles in directed graphs can be used. This can be done using the following data structures:

(1) For each process, a list of the resources it holds.
(2) For each resource, a list of the processes that are waiting for it, and an indication of which process is actually using it.

A check for deadlock can be made at each resource request (or less frequently, depending on how likely it is to arise). Checking on each request has the advantage of early detection, but on the other hand, less frequent checks consume less processor time and may therefore be preferable. If deadlocks are very infrequent, the operator may be relied on to do the detection and the recovery.

If checking is being done at every resource request, then it becomes necessary, before halting process P for resource R, to check that this does not lead to a circular wait condition. A simple recursive algorithm will check this, as follows:

```
PROCEDURE check deadlock (p : process, r : resource)
  FOR all resources r' held by p DO
  FOR all processes p' halted for r' DO
    IF p' holds r THEN there is a deadlock
      ELSE check deadlock (p', r)
```

If checking is being done only periodically, then it is necessary to repeat this check for *all* resources. Note that the algorithm can be coded far more efficiently by tagging processes once they have been checked, so that there is no need to check them again.

Once a deadlock has occurred, an attempt must be made to recover the situation. This is likely to be quite drastic, involving termination of at least one of the deadlocked processes, or preempting resources. Whether or not this is a satisfactory way of dealing with deadlocks depends on the frequency with which they arise and the cost and acceptability of the recovery measures. In some cases an occasional process lost (or restarted from the beginning) may be perfectly acceptable so long as it does not happen too often. In other cases it might be disastrous.

8.2.3 Deadlock avoidance

The avoidance technique involves dynamically deciding whether allocating a resource will lead to a deadlock situation. There are two common strategies that can be employed:

(1) Do not start a process if its demands might force a deadlock situation.
(2) Habermann's Algorithm (Habermann, 1969), also known as the 'Banker's Algorithm'.

Before considering the operation of these algorithms, suitable notation must be defined. Consider a system running n processes, and with m different types of resources. Let

Vector $\mathbf{a} = \begin{pmatrix} a_1 \\ \cdot \\ \cdot \\ \cdot \\ a_m \end{pmatrix}$ gives the total amount of each resource in the system

Matrix $\mathbf{B} = \begin{pmatrix} b_{11} \cdot \cdot \cdot b_{n1} \\ \cdot \qquad \cdot \\ \cdot \qquad \cdot \\ \cdot \qquad \cdot \\ b_{1m} \cdot \cdot \cdot b_{nm} \end{pmatrix} = (\mathbf{b}_1, \mathbf{b}_2, \mathbf{b}_3, \dots \mathbf{b}_n)$

gives the requirements of each process for each resource. That is, $b_{ij} =$ maximum requirement of process i for resource j (assuming that this information is known when the process is started).

$$\text{Matrix } C = \begin{pmatrix} c_{11} \cdots c_{n1} \\ \cdot \\ \cdot \\ \cdot \\ c_{1m} \cdots c_{nm} \end{pmatrix} = (c_1, c_2, c_3, \ldots c_n)$$

gives the current allocations. That is, c_{ij} = amount of each resource j allocated to process i.

Obviously:

(1) For all k, $b_k \leq a$ (no process can claim more resources than the total available)

(2) For all k, $c_k \leq b_k$ (no process is allocated more than its total maximum requirement)

(3) $\sum_{k=1}^{n} c_k \leq a$ (at most all resources are allocated)

One possible strategy which cannot deadlock, is to start a new process P_{n+1} only if

$$a \geq \sum_{k=1}^{n} b_k + b_{n+1}$$

That is, process P_{n+1} is started only if its requirements can be fully satisfied should all processes claim their maximum requirements. This strategy is less than optimal as it assumes that all processes will make their maximum demand together. In general they will not do so, and

$$c_k \ll b_k$$

8.2.4 The Banker's Algorithm

In order to implement this allocation algorithm correctly, it requires that:

(1) The maximum resource requirement of each process is stated in advance (for example, when the process is created).

(2) The processes under consideration are independent (that is, the order in which they execute is immaterial; there are no synchronisation constraints).

(3) There are no real-time constraints; that is, it must be acceptable for a process to be held up for long periods whenever it makes a resource

request. (In systems of cooperating processes, this can be relaxed if it is known that all processes hold resources for only a short time.)

Provided that these conditions are satisfied, the following resource allocation strategy (process P requesting resource R) can be applied.

(1) Use the Banker's Algorithm to determine whether allocating R to P will result in an unsafe state.

(2) If so, halt P; otherwise, allocate R to P.

A safe state is one in which there is at least one order in which the processes can be run which does not result in a deadlock. Let such a sequence be

$$S = P_{s1}, P_{s2}, ... P_{sn}$$

That is, P_{s1} is run, then P_{s2} and so on. The state must be safe if deadlock will not occur even in the worst case (all processes request their maximum allocations).

For this to be true, the resources available

$$(a - \sum_{k=1}^{n} c_k) \geq b_{s1} - c_{s1} \text{ to allow } P_{s1} \text{ to run.}$$

After P_{s1} has run its resources c_{s1} will be freed, so for P_{s2}

$$a - \sum_{k=1}^{n} c_k + c_{s1} \geq b_{s2} - c_{s2}$$

In general, a sequence S must exist such that for all processes P_k, the total resources minus the resources currently allocated to all processes after P_k in the sequence must be $\leq b_k$ (= maximum requirement for P_k). A resource request can be granted without the danger of deadlocks only if the resultant state is safe, otherwise the requesting process must be halted until more resources become available.

Having established that a safe sequence exists, it is not necessary deliberately to run processes in that sequence - once a deadlock situation is approached, a safe sequence will be enforced as a result of more processes becoming halted.

To prove that a state is safe, a sequence must be found that satisfies the resource allocation conditions specified above. However, there are $n!$ possible sequences, and it would be impractical to try them all. Fortunately, if several processes can be run first, then so far as this algorithm is concerned, it does not matter which is actually chosen first. This means that a safe sequence can be determined as follows:

(1) Find any P_k that can be completed.
(2) Assume that P_k is completed and release its resources.
(3) If any more processes are left - repeat from (1).

If at stage (1) no process P_k can be completed, that state is unsafe.

In some cases this solution to the deadlock problem is not completely satisfactory. The insistence of the Banker's Algorithm on independent processes may be unrealistic. Furthermore, in many cases, a near-deadlock can be almost as undesirable as a deadlock, as it forces the system to stop multiprogramming and may drastically affect performance. Thus there are other practical measures that may be applied as well as, or in some cases, instead of those given above. These are mainly of a 'tuning' nature and involve adjustment of parameters to ensure that deadlocks are extremely unlikely to arise. For example, a system may stop accepting jobs when the amount of free backing store is low, or cease scheduling certain classes of jobs when resources are heavily utilised.

In order to illustrate the use of the Banker's Algorithm, we can regard the three parameters in terms of:

AVAILABLE   the vector **(a)** to represent the amount of resource available

CLAIMS   the matrix **(B)** to represent the amount of each of the resources that each of the processes requires

ALLOCATED   the matrix **(C)** to represent the amount of each of the resources currently allocated to each of the processes.

Consider a simple example where there is only one type of resource, so that AVAILABLE has a single entry showing 12 units of that resource available. Consider also the state where there are three processes P1, P2 and P3, holding resources. CLAIMS and ALLOCATED may appear as follows:

	Process P1	Process P2	Process P3
CLAIMS	5	9	7
ALLOCATED	4	6	0

In order to complete, each process would require the additional resources given by (CLAIMS - ALLOCATED), namely

P1 needs 1
P2 needs 3
P3 needs 7

At this time, 10 units have been allocated out of a maximum potential of 12, so there are only a further 2 units that can be allocated. By the algorithm, there is only one possible safe sequence, namely P1, P2, P3.

The processes are not required to run in this order, and in principle, a further unit may be allocated to any of the three processes and a safe sequence will still remain. However, one of the remaining two units *must* be allocated to P1 to enable it to finish. If requests come from P2 or P3 for both of the remaining two units, the request would be withheld, as a safe sequence would no longer exist and deadlock would ensue.

Once P1 has finished, it releases 5 units of resource back into AVAIL-ABLE. Still there is only one safe sequence, namely P2, P3. This means that ultimately enough resources should be allocated to P2 to enable it to finish next.

This example is for the simple case of a single type of resource, and in general, data structures such as AVAILABLE will be multi-element vectors and the allocation algorithm will be less straightforward in its operation.

8.3 Summary

Most functions of an operating system are concerned with the allocation of resources. Strategies for resource allocation are required to be fair, efficient and accountable, but above all they must be 'safe'. It would be intolerable to have a system where requests by users or their processes might never be serviced. Problems arise with resource allocation when multiple processes are competing for control of the same set of resources. Issues, such as 'fairness' in allocating the resources, are relatively easy to address using information about previous resource usage, process priority etc. However, a situation may arise where a number of processes are waiting for resources currently held by other waiting processes, such that no process may proceed. This situation is known as a deadlock and may be viewed as an unsafe state for the system.

This chapter has examined the criteria for the occurrence of deadlocks within a system. Three possible solutions have been presented. The first, deadlock prevention, involves constraining the system design so that one of the deadlock criteria would never arise. The second, detection and recovery, assumes that deadlock situations may arise, albeit infrequently, so the most effective strategy for managing them is to detect their occurrence and take remedial action, such as faulting a process. The third solution is deadlock avoidance, which involves predicting when a deadlock is liable to occur at the time when resources are requested. The request can therefore be delayed until resources are released and the potential for deadlock no longer exists. Deadlock avoidance, although effective, requires prior knowledge of future resource requirements and so may be used in deterministic systems only.

8.4 References and bibliography

P. Brinch Hansen (1977). *The Architecture of Concurrent Programs*, Prentice-Hall, Englewood Cliffs, N.J.

E.G. Coffman, M. Elphick and A. Shoshani (1971). 'System Deadlocks', *Computing Surveys*, Vol. 3, pp. 67-78.

D.J. Frailey (1973). 'A Practical Approach to Managing Resources and Avoiding Deadlocks', *Communications of the ACM*, Vol. 16, No. 5, pp. 323-9.

A.N. Habermann (1969). 'Prevention of System Deadlocks', *Communications of the ACM*, Vol. 12, pp. 373-85.

A.N. Habermann (1978). 'System Deadlocks', *Current Trends in Programming Methodology*, Vol. III, Prentice-Hall, Englewood Cliffs, N.J., pp. 256-97.

C.A.R. Hoare (1978). 'Communicating Sequential Processes', *Communications of the ACM*, Vol. 21, pp. 666-7.

SS. Isloor and T.A. Marsland (1980). 'The Deadlock Problem: An Overview', *Computer*, Vol. 13, No. 9, pp. 58-78.

9 Resource Management - Protection

9.1 Introduction to protection systems

In chapter 8 one of the major problems of resource allocation, that of processes deadlocking, was considered. In this chapter the second major problem will be considered, that of control of access to the resources - that is, controlling *who* can perform *which operations* and on *which objects*.

Protection systems have mainly evolved in connection with areas or segments of store, with other resources being managed in more or less *ad hoc* ways. However, some of the more general protection systems are suitable for managing all of the resources of a computer system. The requirement for protection arose initially in order to protect the operating system against its users - that is, to prevent a user process from overwriting its code and data, and from taking control of its devices. Thus the emphasis in protection systems was on restricting the operations that a user could perform. Earlier chapters on store management showed how this could be implemented using base-limit registers or similar paging hardware. Most of the protection systems in use today reflect this, in that they recognise two distinct 'execution states', *user* and *supervisor* (different systems use different terms for the two states). In supervisor state, everything is permitted; in user state, some restrictions are enforced.

With the development of multiprogramming systems, there arose also a need to protect independent user computations from one another. However, the two-state systems developed for protecting the operating system were sufficient for this. In principle, a privileged operating system is able to implement any required degree of inter-user protection. Thus, for example, quite complex mechanisms can be devised and implemented to allow users to share one another's files in a controlled manner.

The problem with this philosophy is that, as operating systems increase in size and complexity, it has become quite likely that the operating system itself will contain errors. If the whole of the operating system was privileged, then an error in any part of it could cause trouble. This led to the desire to protect *parts* of the operating system from other parts, and so more complex protection

125

systems recognising more than two states were developed. The first major system to incorporate many protection states was MULTICS. For a detailed description of MULTICS, see Organick, (1972). In MULTICS the protection states were ordered into a hierarchy, from most privileged to least privileged, the idea being that only small parts of the operating system would run at the most privileged levels.

A further major development in protection resulted from a desire to produce more symmetrical protection systems. Up to this point, protection tended to work in a hierarchical fashion, so that A might be protected from B, but B was not protected from A. This sufficed for protection within the operating system, although many people observed that the modular structure of an operating system did not really give rise to a hierarchy of privilege. However, as the use of computers increased, cooperation between users in the form of sharing programs and files became more common and in this context it became highly desirable to allow two programs to cooperate even when neither one trusted the other. This led to the development of the non-hierarchical protection system that permitted the safe cooperation of mutually suspicious programs.

9.2 A general model of protection systems

A protection system manages the control of access to resources. More specifically, it is concerned with two kinds of entity:

(1) *Objects* - the resources to be protected. Associated with each object is a *type* (for example, process, file, printer, etc.) which determines the set of *operations* that may be performed on it (for example, start, kill, read, delete, print, etc.).

(2) *Subjects* - the individuals wishing to access (that is, perform operations on) objects. Depending on the system, subjects may be users, processes, procedures, etc.

The function of a protection system is to define and enforce a set of access rules, just as encountered with segment and file accesses. The access rules may be regarded as relations between subjects and objects: associated with each (subject, object) pair is an *access right* which defines the set of operations that this particular subject may perform on this particular object. Obviously an access right may specify a subset of the total set of operations defined on an object, as determined by its type. Normally we shall be interested in subjects that are *processes*. The set of objects that a process can access at any given time is referred to as its *domain*. In describing a particular system, the following must be defined:

(1) How the domain of a process is represented in the protection system and how the protection rules are actually enforced.

(2) Under what circumstances, and in what ways, a process can move from one domain to another - that is, can it gain and lose access rights as a result of executing certain types of operation?

9.2.1 Defining and representing domains

There are many ways in which the access rules may be represented and these give rise to different kinds of protection systems. Perhaps the most obvious representation is in the form of an *access matrix* that holds the rights for each (subject, object) pair.

	Object A	Object B
Subject 1	Read Write	
Subject 2	Read	Read Write

Figure 9.1   Domain access matrix

The situation shown in figure 9.1 would allow subject 1 to perform READ and WRITE operations on object A, and no operations at all on object B; subject 2 has READ permission for object A, and READ and WRITE permission for object B. In practice, the rights would probably be encoded as bit patterns, but even so, the access matrix would most likely be both large and sparse and so alternative methods of representation are normally used.

The most common sparse matrix representations are to store the matrix separately by row or by column, and these form two common protection systems. Storing by row gives, for each subject, a list of the rights of that subject to the various objects. The above access matrix:

SUBJECT 1:   OBJECT A(READ, WRITE)
SUBJECT 2:   OBJECT A(READ); OBJECT B(READ, WRITE)

Rights expressed in this form are called *capabilities* (Dennis and Van Horn, 1966, Fabry, 1974). A protection system based on capabilities gives each subject a list of capabilities, one for each object it may access, and requires that the appropriate capability be presented to the subject each time that an object is accessed. The capability is regarded as a 'ticket of authorisation' to access; ownership of a capability implies the right to access. How this works will be explained later. As a simple example, the segment table in a segmented system is in effect a capability list and each entry is a capability. However, the term 'capability system' is usually reserved for systems that take advantage of the capability structure to provide a general means for defining and changing domains within a process.

Storing the access matrix by columns gives a list of the subjects that may access each object. Using the same example:

OBJECT A: SUBJECT 1 (READ, WRITE); SUBJECT 2 (READ)
OBJECT B: SUBJECT 2 (READ, WRITE)

This representation is called an *access list*, or *access control list* (ACL) and is quite commonly used in file directories. Although UNIX itself only supports the (user, group, others) concept for file protection, we can postulate a possible way that an ACL might be implemented in UNIX-like file system. The simplest approach would be to put the ACL for each file into a separate disk block and then include that block number in the i-node for that file. The domain could then be specified by the user-id (uid), group-id (gid) pair. If there were three users, John, Jane and Fred, who belong to the groups system, staff and student respectively, four files might have the following ACLs:

File0:   (John, *, rwx)
File1:   (John, system, rwx)
File2:   (Jane, *, rw-), (Fred, student, r--)
File3:   (*, student, r--)

Each ACL entry in parentheses specifies a uid, gid and an allowed access. An asterisk means all uids or gids as appropriate. This would be interpreted as:

File0   read, write and execute access to anyone with the uid = John and gid = any gid.

File1   read, write and execute access for anyone with uid = John and gid = system.

File2   read and write access to anyone with uid = Jane and gid = any gid, and also read only access for anyone with uid = Fred and gid = student.

File3   read only access to anyone with uid = any uid and gid = student.

The system so far described is the basis of the MULTICS system. The nature of ACLs is modified in UNIX, as described in chapter 7, where the file access is specified by 9 bits that represent the rwx access per file for the owner, owner's group and others.

Capability lists and access lists are, in a sense, the two 'pure' representations of the protection rules. Each has its own particular advantages.

Capabilities allow rigid checking of access rights, as the appropriate rights are presented by the subject on each access, but make it rather difficult for the owner of an object to revoke or change the rights given to others (as the capabilities are stored with the subjects rather than the objects). Access lists tend to give slower checking as a search is required to find the appropriate right, but do allow much easier alteration of rights. Consequently, some systems use a combined technique. For example, a file directory may contain access lists, which are checked only on opening a file. If the file is successfully opened, a capability for it is generated and used in all further accesses by this process. Since this kind of capability lasts only for the duration of a job, there is no difficulty in deleting or changing rights.

There is a third method of representing protection information. This is referred to as a 'lock-and-key' system and is quite commonly used because it leads to an extremely efficient access authorisation procedure. It involves associating a 'lock' (effectively, a sort of password) with each object and giving a 'key' to each subject authorised to use the object. The key must be presented on every access to the object, and the access is allowed only if the key matches the lock. Unlike a capability, the key does not identify a particular resource uniquely; several resources tend to be grouped together and given the same key because locks and keys are usually restricted in size to obtain an efficient hardware implementation. Thus lock-and-key systems tend to be rather less general but potentially more efficient than the other two methods.

An example of a lock-and-key system is the MULTICS hierarchical protection system. This deals with the access rights of processes (subjects) to segments (objects). All the segments accessible to a process are described by entries in its segment table which thus acts as a kind of capability list. However, associated with each segment (in its segment table entry) is a 4-bit lock. The 4-bit key is held in the processor status register and defines the currently active domain. Access to the segment is permitted provided that the value of the key is not greater than the value of the lock.

Thus, *within each process* there is a *hierarchy* of sixteen domains corresponding to the sixteen possible key values. With key zero, everything can be accessed. With key 1, everything except segments with lock = 0 can be accessed, and so on. This is a generalisation of the two-level protection schemes commonly employed on conventional systems.

It should be noted that the precise definition of a 'matching' key in a lock-and-key system determines the number of domains and the relations between them. For example, with a 4-bit lock-and-key system any of the following could be used:

(1) Key $\leq$ Lock. This gives sixteen hierarchically ordered domains such that the access rights of domain i are a subset of those of domains 0 ... i-1.

(2) Key = Lock. This gives sixteen non-overlapping domains - that is, there are no common resources between the domains.

(3) (Lock AND Key) $<>$ 0. That is, some bits set in both lock and key. This again gives sixteen domains, but with only a partial ordering between domains, so that some domains are disjointed while others overlap with one another.

9.3 Inter-domain transitions

So far several different ways in which protection domains can be defined and represented in a computer system have been described. However, it is also necessary to identify exactly how a process can transfer between different domains in the course of execution. The 'ideal' would be to enable the process at any instant to have access only to those objects that it needs in order to perform its current task. This implies a very high rate of switching between domains, say on every procedure call.

Protection systems can be loosely classified into three types according to how domain changes are achieved. In the simplest type of system, a process cannot switch between domains and the access rights change only on switching to another process. The most general type of system permits arbitrary changes between domains on each procedure call, allowing the 'ideal' mentioned above to be achieved. Such systems are usually based on capabilities, as these are the only representation that can efficiently support such a general system. The third kind of system allows changes of domain on procedure calling, but restricts the kind of domain change allowed. These are usually based on lock-and-key representation systems and the restrictions depend on the particular choice of lock and key. Restricted systems are attractive in spite of the fact that they cannot achieve the 'ideal', because they can at least be built at a reasonable cost.

The three types of system are discussed in more detail below.

9.3.1 Domain changes only on process changes

This is a static kind of protection system that can be implemented with simple two-state (user/supervisor) machines as it requires only a means of separating processes from one another. On the whole it is quite adequate for protecting user processes from one another, but tends to lead to a large and privileged operating system.

If it is required to protect parts of the operating system from one another, then it is necessary effectively to run each module as though it were a separate process. Then, only a small part of the system (a kernel, responsible for dealing with protecting and multiprogramming processes) needs to be privileged. However, the other modules (including user jobs) need a means of communicating with one another and so a message system must be provided by the kernel to allow this. Processes (modules) then communicate by passing messages to one another. This, in theory, can give a completely safe and general protection system by isolating each small operating system function within its own protected 'virtual machine'. However, the message and process changing costs can be high if the partitioning into virtual machines is taken too far!

9.3.2 Restricted domain change systems

In this class of system, each process has a restricted set of domains associated with it (as determined by the key values of a lock-and-key domain system) and a controlled means is provided for switching between domains on certain procedure calls. While not completely general, they do permit some distinction in the accessing of rights for different parts of a process. As a practical example of this kind of system, the MULTICS hierarchical protection system (Schroeder and Salzer, 1972) will now be considered.

As mentioned previously, MULTICS uses a lock-and-key representation for domains. The system is primarily concerned with controlling access to segments and so the lock is a 4-bit number held in the segment table entry for each segment. The 4-bit key is held in the processor status register and defines the currently active domain. As described earlier, hierarchical access control may be permitted to a segment provided that the current key value is not greater than the lock for the segment; further access bits then determine the kind of accesses that can be made (for example Read, Write and Execute). So, the access check procedure on each access to the store can be described as:

IF pstatus.key ≤ segtable[s].lock

   AND requiredoperation ≤ segtable[s].accessrights

   THEN {access to segment s is permitted}

This enables each process to have sixteen domains, corresponding to the sixteen different key values, and to arrange the domains in a hierarchy from most privileged (key = 0) to least privileged (key = 15).

Clearly, for the protection system to operate, the user must be restricted from accessing the processor status register. If the user could write arbitrary values into the KEY field of this register, then the protection system is completely useless. In fact, the KEY field can be changed only indirectly as a result of calling a procedure in a different segment, and hence possibly in a different domain. When this is done, the hardware first checks that the call is legal (that is, it satisfies the protection rules) and then changes the key value if necessary.

Procedure calling is controlled by an extra access control bit, in addition to the normal READ, WRITE and EXECUTE permissions, that defines a permission to 'CALL' a procedure within a segment. The hardware action on calling a new procedure p in a new segment s is:

IF pstatus.key $\leq$ segtable[s].lock
   AND call $\leq$ segtable[s].accessrights
   AND p is a valid entry point to the segment
   THEN pstatus.key := segtable[s].newkey
         segtable[s].rights := segtable[s].rights + execute

Note that three separate checks are required:

(1) that the present domain can access the segment at all (pstatus.key $\leq$ segtable[s].lock);
(2) that it has permission to CALL procedures in the segment (call $\leq$ segtable[s].accessrights);
(3) that the point to be entered is a valid procedure entry point (one possible check that could be used is that the entry point is in the first n locations of the segment).

The last check is important, as arbitrary damage can be caused if a privileged procedure is entered at some undefined point rather than at its start.

In the course of entering the procedure, the hardware must also set the KEY to the appropriate value for the called procedure (from the segment table), and set Execute permission in the rights for the segment to allow code to be executed in the segment subsequently. (Thus, even if the segment did not originally have execute permission, provided that it is CALLed at a valid point it can be executed.)

The main problems with this kind of organisation are:

(1) Validation of reference parameters - when a procedure A is calling a procedure B, it is possible to pass a pointer that is accessible to B but not to A. Strictly, such a call should be made illegal.

(2) Call to less privileged procedures (including procedures supplied as parameters to more privileged procedures). Here, the less privileged procedure cannot be given access to the caller's stack and so a new stack in a new segment must be created for the duration of the call. This in turn complicates parameter passing and in many systems, a call to a less privileged procedure is deemed illegal.

(3) The restriction of domains being in a hierarchy means that general problems, such as the cooperation of mutually suspicious procedures, cannot be solved.

9.3.3 Arbitrary domain changes

Systems permitting arbitrary changes of domain are generally implemented using capabilities, since lock-and-key systems cannot support arbitrary domains and access control lists are slow in use. For an efficient system, hardware implementation of capabilities is essential.

A capability is a ticket authorising its holder to access some object. In general, a capability needs to give three items of information about the object:

(1) The TYPE of the object - for example, SEGMENT, PRINTER, FILE, etc. The type of an object defines which operations make sense on it.

(2) The IDENTIFICATION of a particular object.

(3) The ACCESS RIGHTS to the object - that is, the subset of the operations defined for this particular object type that the capability authorises the holder to perform.

To prevent the user from generating arbitrary capabilities, which would obviously totally invalidate the protection system, capabilities are normally held together in a capability segment. This is like a normal segment except that it does not have the usual read, write or execute permissions. Instead, it has the access permissions READ CAPABILITY and WRITE CAPABILITY, allowing the process to use its contents as capabilities (but not data) and to store capabilities (but not data) into it. The current 'domain' will be defined by such a capability segment: any objects for which the current capability segment contains a capability can be accessed but other objects cannot. Thus, changing from one domain to another involves altering the hardware register that points to the current capability segment (in this context, 'points' actually means 'contains a capability for').

As always, of course, changes of domain need to be carefully controlled as a process cannot be allowed to change its domain without somehow checking that the change is a valid one. As with the MULTICS system, this checking is achieved by binding domain changes to the procedure call operation so that a change of domain can occur only on switching to a new procedure. Again, a new type of access right, CALL, is introduced to control the operation of calling a 'protected' procedure (that is, one requiring a domain change). Corresponding to this is a hardware procedure call instruction, which has as its operand (a capability describing) a new capability segment. The call procedure operation can be defined as:

call procedure (s)

        IF s.type = segment
        AND call ≤ s.accessrights
        THEN currentdomain := s
            set readcapability and writecapability permission
                into currentdomain.accessrights
            set currentproceduresegment := first capability in segment s
            (effectively, a jump)

The following points are worth noting as compared with the MULTICS system. Firstly, the need explicitly to check whether the current domain is permitted to access the procedure specified is no longer necessary. The fact that the current domain can produce a capability for the procedure means that it must be allowed to access the procedure. There is, however, an extra type checking operation if capabilities are used to describe resources other than segments. Also, there is no longer the need to index into a segment table to check the access rights - they are already there in the capability presented (which presumably has already been taken out of the caller's capability segment, in effect a segment table). The domain change operation involves setting the hardware 'current capability segment' register and augmenting its access rights to include READ and WRITE CAPABILITY, and then entering the procedure. Once again, if it were required to pack more than one procedure into a segment, then a 'valid entry point' check would be needed, as in the MULTICS system.

In the relatively simple system described above, a total change of domain occurs on entering a protected procedure. No objects are common to the two domains unless they are explicitly placed in the called domain prior to the call, and allowing this would be dangerous. In a practical system, therefore, the current domain is represented by several capability segments, not just one. The Cambridge CAP computer recognised four distinct components of the current domain:

(1) Global data, which is not changed at all on a protected procedure call - that is, it is common to all domains.

(2) Local data, which is created afresh within the called procedure on each activation.

(3) Own data, which 'belongs' to the procedure and retains its values even when the procedure is not active. This is changed on every protected procedure call in the manner described above.

(4) Parametric data, which is passed from the caller to the called procedure.

Thus the current domain is represented by four capabilities, two of which are changed on a protected procedure call [(3) and (4)].

9.4 An example of a capability system

Capability systems can provide the mechanism whereby processes can switch between a set of arbitrary domains in a completely controlled manner. Using them, it is possible to implement the 'ideal' of giving a process access only to those objects that it needs to perform its current task. However, such systems introduce new problems - for example, how are protected procedures actually created? Ideally users would be able to create them but obviously there must be some control over this. A system called HYDRA will now be considered; developed at Carnegie-Mellon University, it illustrates how some of these problems can be solved. It is described in detail in Wulf et al. (1981).

Consider a file system in which files are protected by capabilities. The operations on files implemented by this basic file system might be:

READ_BLOCK, which reads a specified block of the file
WRITE_BLOCK, which writes a specified block to the file
DELETE, which deletes the file

Now suppose that a new kind of file is to be created using the above basic file system. This new file is a SEQFILE or sequential file, to which the following operations apply:

READ_NEXT_CHARACTER
WRITE_NEXT_CHARACTER
APPEND_CHARACTER (adds a character to the end of the file)
DELETE

With such a set of operations, files could be created that can only be read character by character, or that can only be added to at the end.

A capability for a SEQFILE will have TYPE = 'SEQFILE', and the access rights will be some subset of those given above. However, the actual object itself will be a file in the basic file system and the only operations that are permitted on it are READ_BLOCK, WRITE_BLOCK and DELETE. The procedure that implements the READ_CHARACTER operation will need to be able to change the capability so that its type is 'FILE' and its access rights include READ_BLOCK. This is known as an access amplification and is obviously a highly dangerous operation that must be carefully controlled. Before it can be discussed further, the concept of type as it applies to a protection system must be considered in more detail.

9.4.1 Types and access amplification

It has already been said that the type of an object defines the set of operations that can be performed on it. For a static system, in which 'user' and 'system' are well-defined terms, this is sufficient. The user asks to perform an operation, the system interprets the access rights to check if the operation is allowed and, if so, performs the operation.

A problem arises when the idea of the 'system' as a static, monolithic entity is dropped. In the above example, an attempt was made to extend the system in such a way that

(1) the extensions were themselves fully protected - that is, they would be as secure as the rest of the system - but

(2) the extensions did not in any way compromise the security of the existing system. That is, even if the SEQFILE implementation was incorrect it could not possibly break any of the protection rules relating to the existing object type FILE.

This kind of extension is obviously essential if arbitrarily complex systems are to be built in a systematic way such that additions cannot wreck the operation of parts that already work.

Once the idea of building a system as a sort of hierarchy of subsystems, as above, is accepted, a more carefully defined concept of type is needed. The type of an object must now define both

(1) what the object actually consists of - that is, how it is implemented - and

(2) what operations can be performed on it.

If a new type of object is defined, saying what it consists of and what operations are valid on it, then procedures can be written to perform these operations. It is here that both access checking and access amplification are required. Checking is needed to ensure that the operation about to be performed is actually allowed, and amplification has to obtain for the operation-defining procedure the rights that it needs to perform the operation.

Amplification is achieved by an operation AMPLIFY with two parameters. The first is the capability to be altered and the second is a capability for a special kind of object called an amplification template. The template is the means of controlling access amplification, and gives:

(1) The TYPE of object whose access is to be amplified.
(2) The rights that must be present in order for the amplification to work.
(3) The new type that is to be set after amplification.
(4) The new set of rights to be set after amplification.

The operation can then be defined as:

amplify (c,t)

    IF c.type = t.type
        AND t.rights ≤ c.rights
        THEN   c.type := t.newtype
                c.rights := t.newrights

Thus, by calling 'amplify', a procedure will check the access permission on the parameter it has been given and perform the amplification required, provided that it has the suitable template available. For example, the template needed for the READ_NEXT_CHARACTER operation would be:

type	=	seqfile
rights	=	read_next_character
newtype	=	file
newrights	=	read_block

Normally, only the creator of a type would be allowed to create templates for that type, and so the entire mechanism is secure. This control is, of course, also achieved by using capabilities, as outlined below.

9.4.2 Creation of new types

A standard system command NEWTYPE is used to create new object types. This is supplied with:

(a) the name of the type
(b) information about what the type consists of
(c) the names of operations that apply to the type

It returns a new capability for an object of type TYPE, and with access rights CREATE, DELETE, CHANGERIGHTS, TRANSFER and TEMPLATE. The capability is put away in the user's directory for future use. The access rights refer to standard operations defined by the system on objects of type TYPE, as follows:

CREATE(T)   creates a capability for a new object of type T (compare this with NEW in PASCAL).

DELETE(T)   deletes the object.

CHANGERIGHTS   enables a capability to be constructed with access rights that are a subset of those in the given capability. Thus CHANGERIGHTS is not a protection hazard.

TRANSFER   can be used to give access to an object of type T to another user (that is, to place transfer a capability for it). A combination of CHANGERIGHTS followed by TRANSFER can thus be used to give another user a capability with fewer rights than those of the donor.

TEMPLATE   is used to create an amplification template for an object of this type. Normally, the creator of a type will not give any other user a capability containing TEMPLATE rights and so only the creator will be able to create templates for the type.

Returning to the original SEQFILE example, NEWTYPE can be used to create a new type of object called SEQFILE, which consists of a FILE with the operations READ_NEXT_CHARACTER, WRITE_NEXT_CHARACTER, APPEND_CHARACTER defined in addition to the standard operations DELETE, CHANGERIGHTS and TRANSFER. This will give a new capability, with:

type   =   TYPE
identification =   'SEQFILE'
rights   =   {CREATE, DELETE, CHANGERIGHTS,
                    TRANSFER, TEMPLATE}

The TEMPLATE rights can now be used to create amplification templates for the operations READ_NEXT_CHARACTER, WRITE_NEXT_CHARACTER, APPEND_CHARACTER, and these can be used to implement the three operations.

CREATE rights can be used to create a new SEQFILE object, which can then be accessed using the operations READ_NEXT_CHARACTER, WRITE_NEXT_CHARACTER, APPEND_CHARACTER and the standard operations including DELETE. Note that READ_BLOCK or WRITE_BLOCK cannot be used directly unless we cheat and call AMPLIFY directly.

CHANGERIGHTS and TRANSFER can be used to give access to a SEQFILE to someone else. It can also be arranged that they have the same rights or a subset. They can also be used to give someone else access to the type SEQFILE (as distinct from giving them individual SEQFILE objects), but usage of this type would then be rather obscure.

The capability approach clearly has much in common with the now popular paradigm of object-oriented programming. Capabilities could provide a suitable vehicle for implementing objects with appropriate encapsulation and control. However, to provide a rigorous protection system using capabilities requires an efficient implementation in hardware. In practice, few capability machines have been built.

9.5 Summary

This chapter has considered techniques for controlling access to resources, in effect, deciding which subjects can perform which operations on which objects. The set of access rights which are currently applicable is known as the current domain. Two main ways exist of representing a domain. A capability list identifies which objects are accessible to any one subject and an access control list identifies which subjects may access a particular object. Both forms are used within operating systems generally.

The most crucial aspect of any protection system is to provide a controlled means of changing domains so that a different set of access rights apply. Three techniques have been identified. The most simple is to change domains by changing processes. This is the most simple to implement, even with primitive hardware support, although it requires efficient process management to be effective. The second is a restricted form of domain changing, usually implemented by a special form of procedure call and using a simple lock-and-key representation for the domain. The most powerful is to permit arbitrary domain changing using a hardware implementation of capabilities. An example of such a system is presented.

9.6 References and bibliography

D.E. Denning (1982). *Cryptography and Data Security*, Addison-Wesley, Reading, Mass.

J.B.Dennis and E.C. Van Horn (1966). 'Programming Semantics for Multiprogramming Computations', *Communications of the ACM*, Vol. 9, pp. 143-55.

R.S. Fabry (1974), 'Capability Based Addressing', *Communications of the ACM* Vol. 17, pp. 403-12

R.M. Graham (1968). 'Protection in an Information Processing Utility', *Communications of the ACM*, Vol. 11, pp. 365-9.

F.T. Grampp and R.H. Morris (1984). 'UNIX Operating System Security', *AT&T Bell Laboratories Technical Journal*, No. 63, pp. 1649-72.

E.I. Organick (1972). *The MULTICS System*, MIT Press, Boston.

M.D. Schroeder and J.H. Salzer (1972). 'A Hardware Architecture for Implementing Protection Rings', *Communications of the ACM*, Vol. 15, pp. 157-70.

W.A. Wulf, R. Levin and S.P. Harbison (1981), *Hydra/C.mmp: An Experimental Computer System*, McGraw-Hill, New York.

10 Process Synchronisation - Basic Principles

10.1 Introduction

Operating systems have so far tended to be regarded as a set of largely independent processes. After all, the functions that are being performed are clearly defined and largely self-contained. In theory, many of these processes could be run in parallel, and if a multiprocessor system were available, then separate processors could be allocated for them. In a single processor system, the processes have to be multiprogrammed, switching from one process to another according to a suitable scheduling algorithm.

In practice, the processes that constitute an operating system cannot be totally independent. For example, in the simple system outlined in chapter 2, the terminal manager has to pass characters to the job processor according to mutually agreed conventions, for example, individually when they are typed or one line at a time. Therefore, there has to be a mechanism for *communication* between processes. The obvious solution to this (and the one most commonly adopted) is a shared data structure. In the example, this might be a buffer as described in chapter 3, where characters are inserted by the terminal manager and removed by the job processor. There are certain (obvious) rules that have to be obeyed with this type of communication:

(1) Information cannot be removed from the buffer until it has been placed there.
(2) Information placed in the buffer must not be overwritten with new information before it has been used.

In order to be able to conform to these rules, the processes may also need to share certain control variables, such as a count of characters. (In this particular example, which might employ circular buffering, the count could probably be deduced from the buffer pointer variables.) In general, accesses to both the shared control variables and the main data structures are potentially very error-prone, and faults in the communication between operating system processes will have a disastrous effect on the performance and reliability of the computer system. There are two main problem areas:

(1) process synchronisation

(2) process competition

It will be shown that dependent processes can be cooperating, competing or both.

10.1.1 Process synchronisation

Processes must be able to inform one another that they have completed a certain action. This is necessary to satisfy the requirements for a communication system, namely that information must not be overwritten before the old information has been consumed, and that no attempt should be made to remove information before it has been made available. For example, in the first case, the terminal manager might test the variable char_count against some suitable limit, using a sequence such as

IF char_count = buffer_size THEN wait for prod

The terminal manager can do nothing more until it receives a prod from the job processor to say that characters have been removed and space is now available in the buffer. A similar test and prodding mechanism is also necessary to test for an empty buffer.

10.1.2 Process competition

Whenever there are two processes trying to access a shared variable, there is a danger that the variable will be updated wrongly owing to peculiarities in the timing of the memory accesses. For example, again considering the terminal manager and job processor concurrently accessing char_count, the actions they might perform are:

Terminal Manager   char_count := char_count + 1
Job Processor   char_count := char_count − 1

If these processes are running in separate processors, which by chance try to execute these operations simultaneously, depending on which one completes last, the resulting values of char_count will be either one too many or one too few. In the first case the system has apparently gained a character, whereas in the second case it has lost one.

A similar effect can occur in a single processor system where processes are being multiprogrammed. Consider a machine with a single accumulator (ACC), the actual machine instructions that are obeyed to perform these operations might be of the form:

Job Processor	Terminal Manager
ACC = char_count	ACC = char_count
ACC = ACC – 1	ACC = ACC + 1
ACC => char_count	ACC => char_count

Hence, process changing in the middle of these sequences can result in an incorrect value for char_count, as shown below:

Job Processor	Terminal Manager
ACC = char_count	

An interrupt occurs (say) and the job processor is preempted to allow another process to process to service the interrupt. ACC is stored by the coordinator, to be restored the next time that the job processor is entered

The terminal manager is entered to read a character from the device

ACC = char_count
ACC = ACC + 1
ACC => char_count

Eventually the job processor is re-entered and it resumes its execution with a new (incorrect) value in char_count.

ACC = ACC – 1
ACC => char_count

and char_count is now wrong!

From this example it can be seen that competition implies that processes are competing for some shared resource. The one basic rule in the case of competition is:

Only one process at a time should be allowed to access the shared resource.

This is known as *mutual exclusion.* Apart from the synchronisation aspects, two of the other problems associated with mutual exclusion have already been encountered, namely:

(1) allocation - which processes are allowed to access the resource

(2) protection - how to prevent other processes from accessing the resource

These aspects were considered in chapters 8 and 9 on resource allocation. In this chapter the main concern is *how* to achieve mutual exclusion; that is, how to ensure that only one process at a time is doing a particular operation.

10.2 Flags

In order to deal in general with process competition, a means must be available of making arbitrary sections of code mutually exclusive. One way to achieve this in a multiprogramming system is to inhibit all interrupts during the execution of such code, but this is unsatisfactory since

(1) there is no direct equivalent for a multiprocessor system, and
(2) it reduces the ability of the system to respond rapidly to critical events.

The alternative approach is to precede all critical operations by a sequence of code that warns all other processes that someone is already executing a critical sequence. The most immediately obvious technique is to use a flag, thus:

WHILE flag = 0 DO {nothing}
flag := 0

    critical section...

flag := 1

The problem with this is that the first two statements *themselves* constitute a critical section and require mutual exclusion, otherwise two processes could simultaneously find the flag non-zero and enter their critical sections. There is a solution to the mutual exclusion problem using only ordinary test and assignment operations (Dijkstra, 1965), but this will not be considered here. What is really desirable is some operation designed specifically for synchronisation purposes - a synchronising primitive.

The problem with the solution above results from the separation of the two operations: (a) testing the flag and (b) modifying it. Probably the simplest operation that gets around this problem is one that *reads and clears* a variable in a single cycle - that is, so that no other process may access the variable inbetween. Many processors have an instruction in their order code specifically for this reason, although the precise nature of the operation (and the name designated to it) differs between processor manufacturers. The *Read and Clear* (or *Read and Mark, Test and Set*) instruction has the effect of reading a store location into a register and setting the store value to zero. A suitable sequence might therefore be:

WHILE read and clear (flag) = 0 DO {nothing}

     critical section

flag := 1

Now, because of the indivisibility of the read and clear operation, it is certain that only one process at a time can enter the critical region. This solution, however, suffers from two related defects. Firstly, it employs the 'busy' form of waiting - that is, processes waiting to enter critical sections are actively looping while they test the flag. This wastes processor time in a multiprogramming system and memory cycles in the shared store of a multiprocessor system. Secondly, it is possible by chance for some process always to find the flag zero and hence never to enter the critical section if there are many other processes also accessing the flag. Although this may be improbable, the aim should be to make such situations impossible.

To avoid busy waiting, two operations can be introduced:

(1)   block   which halts the current process
(2)   wakeup (p)   which frees process p

In a true multiprocessor system these might be hardware operations that actually halt the processor. In a multiprogramming system they would be implemented by the coordinator performing the transitions RUNNING $\rightarrow$ HALTED and HALTED $\rightarrow$ READY. Using these two operations, the next iteration would be:

WHILE read and clear (flag) = 0 DO block

     critical section....

flag := 1
wake (one of the blocked processes, if any)

Again, errors could occur in this. Firstly, the block operation almost certainly involves updating a shared list of blocked processes for use in the wakeup sequence. This updating is probably fairly complicated and requires mutual exclusion! Secondly, it is possible for the following sequence of events to occur:

Process 1

read and clear (flag)

and find it zero, thus deciding to block.
In the meantime, process 2 which is
executing its critical section at the
time, completes it.

block

Process 2

finish critical section
flag := 1

no processes blocked, so process 2
continues without freeing anyone.

Process 1 can now never be freed, as a process is only ever freed by another
process in its critical section.

10.3   Semaphores

To overcome the problems of synchronisation and mutual exclusion, a
primitive, known as a semaphore, has evolved (Dijkstra, 1968a).

A semaphore (s) is an integer variable on which three operations have been
defined:

(1) Initialisation to a non-negative value
s := initial value

(2) wait(s):
IF s <> 0 THEN s := s − 1
ELSE block process

(3) signal(s):
IF queue empty THEN s := s + 1
ELSE free process

For the time being, assume that the wait and signal operations are
indivisible and that there is no question of two processes simultaneously
incrementing or decrementing a semaphore. Their implementation will be
discussed later.

From the definition of the operations, an important property of
semaphores, called the *semaphore invariant* can be derived. This is true of all
semaphores and can be used to make mathematically precise statements about
process synchronisation.

From the definition, if s is a semaphore, then

value(s) = initial value(s) + number of signals(s)
— number of completed waits(s)

and it can easily be seen that value(s) can never be negative. Thus, abbreviated slightly:

$$iv(s) + ns(s) - nw(s) \geq 0$$

This is the semaphore invariant. The following two simple examples will illustrate its use for showing the correctness of synchronisation.

10.3.1 Mutual exclusion by semaphores

Given the correct implementation (in hardware or software) of semaphores, mutual exclusion can be achieved by using a semaphore s initialised to 1 and surrounding each critical region by:

wait(s)

critical region

signal(s)

It is clear that the number of processes in critical regions is equal to the number that have performed a wait(s) without executing the corresponding signal(s); that is, $nw(s) - ns(s)$. From the semaphore invariant, it can immediately be seen that $nw(s) - ns(s) \leq iv(s)$, and since $iv(s) = 1$ this gives 'number of processes in critical sections ≤ 1', which is, of course, the definition of mutual exclusion.

10.3.2 Process communication using semaphores

Now consider a set of processes communicating via a shared buffer of N locations (such as the terminal manager and job processor in the simple system). Each process that places data into the buffer is called a *producer*; each process removing data is a *consumer*. Two rules can be defined which must be obeyed for satisfactory communication between the processes:

(1) Number of items placed in buffer and not removed must be ≥ 0
(2) Number of items placed in buffer and not removed must be $\leq N$

The two types of process can therefore be implemented using two semaphores:

p   which indicates a free position in the buffer and is initialised to N
c   which indicates data available in the buffer and is initialised to 0

Producer	Consumer
REPEAT	REPEAT
produce item;	wait(c);
wait(p)	take item from buffer;
place item in buffer;	signal(p);
signal(c);	process item;
FOREVER	FOREVER

Looking at the structure of the solution, it is easy to see that

(1) Number of items in buffer $\geq ns(c) - nw(c) = -iv(c) = 0$

(2) Number of items in buffer $\leq nw(p) - ns(p) = iv(p) = N$

So the communication constraints are satisfied.

From these examples it can be seen that, in order to **protect** a critical section of code, matching waits and signals are placed around the section. When using semaphores to **communicate** between processes, the waits and signals are placed in opposite processes.

The semaphore is a fairly primitive operation and, although it has worked well for these two cases, it can be difficult to use in more complicated problems. Hence it is probably best regarded as a low-level facility, used to implement other more manageable synchronisation facilities.

10.4 Implementation of semaphores

The wait and signal operations are performed by the coordinator as it has the task of scheduling processes in a multiprogramming system (or allocating processors in a multiprocessor system). Naturally, it must maintain a list with an entry for each semaphore, as shown in figure 10.1.

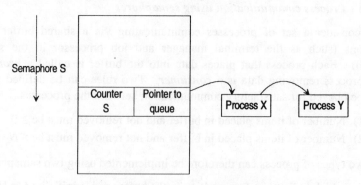

Figure 10.1 List of semaphores

Processes are entered on to the queue when they are blocked during the wait operation, and are removed during the signal operation.

It is through use of the wait and signal procedures that the coordinator knows which processes require to run at any instant in time. The operation of the coordinator can be roughly described as:

REPEAT
    choose the highest priority free process;
    run it until either:
    (a)   it halts (as a result of waiting on a zero-valued semaphore)
    (b)   a higher priority process becomes free
        (as a result of a signal operation).
FOREVER

So far the following logical descriptions have been used as the definitions of wait and signal:

wait(s):

    IF s <> 0 THEN s := s − 1 ELSE block process

signal(s):

    IF queue empty THEN s := s + 1 ELSE free process

A process attempting a WAIT operation on a zero-valued semaphore is thus assumed to be held up until some other process performs a signal. Explicit use has not been made of the value of the semaphore variable (since no operation has been defined that allows this value to be discovered). The only property used is the semaphore invariant:

$$iv(s) + ns(s) - nw(s) \geq 0$$

Any implementation must guarantee that this is always true. It is also essential that the wait and signal operations should be indivisible in order to ensure that it is impossible for (say) two processes simultaneously to find that the semaphore has a value of one and attempt to decrement it. To achieve this, the operations must be implemented using read and clear orders or by inhibiting interrupts. The precise technique depends on whether the operating system is running on a single or multiprocessor system. Each of these cases will now be considered.

10.5 Semaphore implementation for a multiprocessor system

In a true multiprocessor system there are two main approaches to implementing semaphores:

(1) Implement the wait and signal operations directly in hardware, achieving indivisibility by interlocks at the memory interface (for example, by performing the entire operation in a single cycle).

(2) Program the wait and signal operations, using a more basic hardware mechanism (for example, read and clear) to achieve the effect of indivisibility.

10.5.1   Hardware implementation

The fundamental hardware operations that correspond to wait and signal are, respectively:

(a) decrement and test
(b) increment and test

These may be combined with either a goto operation, or suitable blocking operations. For example

wait(s):

IF s := s – 1 < 0 THEN block

signal(s):

IF s := s + 1 ≤ 0 THEN wakeup (one waiting processor)

could be implemented as single, elementary operations. Note that in this case the wakeup operation would pick a processor according to some fairly rigid hardware rule. For this reason semaphores are generally used without making any assumptions about which process will be freed by a signal. The ability to make such assumptions would considerably simplify the solutions of some problems where it is required to give some processes priority over others.

A second point to note is that in this implementation the actual value of the semaphore variable can become negative and, in this case, indicates the number of halted processors. Although it is specified that semaphores take only non-negative values, the synchronisation implied by this implementation is identical with that implied by the logical definition, since a process never passes a wait operation if the value of the semaphore is zero or negative. More formally, if the 'value' of the semaphore s is defined to be IF s ≥ 0 THEN s ELSE 0, it is easy to see that the semaphore invariant

$$value(s) = iv(s) + ns(s) - nw(s) \geq 0$$

still holds, and since this is the *only* property of semaphore that has been used, the synchronisation should still be correct.

10.5.2 Software implementation

If the hardware does not perform the complete operation as above, then obviously some of it has to be programmed in software. This requires some means of ensuring mutual exclusion (that is, indivisibility) during the semaphore operations. If the read and clear operation is available in hardware, the following implementation will suffice:

wait(s):

    WHILE read and clear(flag) = 0 DO {nothing}
    s := s − 1
    IF s < 0 THEN
        BEGIN
        add current process to s.queue
        block {must also set flag back nonzero}
        END
    ELSE
        flag := 1

signal(s):

    WHILE read and clear(flag) = 0 DO {nothing}
    s := s + 1
    IF s ≤ 0 THEN
        BEGIN
        remove one process (p) from s.queue
        wakeup (p)
        END
    flag := 1

where s is the count used to represent the semaphore value, and s.queue is a queue of processes halted on the semaphore s. Note that if s < 0 then (−s) is the number of processes on s.queue.

The variable flag is used to guarantee mutual exclusion while accessing the semaphore. A separate flag could be used for each semaphore but it is unlikely that this would be worth while. Note also that the block operation must also release the mutual exclusion by setting flag non-zero.

'Busy waiting' is used in the case of accesses to flag, but not for halting on the semaphore itself. The flag is only held zero for a very short time and so busy waiting should not occur often or for long. Although it would be possible to replace the block with an equivalent 'busy wait', this would be unacceptable since processes may wait for a considerable length of time.

In the absence of an operation such as read and clear, some other basic mutual exclusion mechanism, such as the one discussed by Dijkstra, would have to be used.

10.6 Semaphore implementation for multiprogramming systems

In a single-processor multiprogramming system, semaphore implementation can be simplified by inhibiting interrupts to obtain mutual exclusion. Thus all operations on flag in the above section are replaced as appropriate by the inhibiting and enabling of interrupts. Busy waiting is clearly unacceptable in this case as it would tie up the one and only available processor, preventing any other process from resetting the flag to 1. Block and wakeup are, of course, procedures implemented by the coordinator rather than hardware operations. They might therefore be implemented as follows:

wait (s):

    inhibit interrupts
    s := s − 1
    IF s < 0 THEN
        add current process to queue s
        block the process and allow interrupts
    ELSE
        allow interrupts

signal (s):

    inhibit interrupts
    s := s + 1
    IF s ≤ 0 THEN
        remove first process (p)
        wakeup (p)
    allow interrupts

While it is not acceptable in general to achieve mutual exclusion by inhibiting interrupts, the semaphore operations could be regarded as an exception, particularly as they are comparatively short.

10.7 The use of semaphores - the reader's and writer's problem

Consider the problem in which:

    (1) Several concurrent processes wish to access a common file.
    (2) Some wish to read; some wish to write.

(3) Shared read accesses to the file are required, but exclusive access is required for the writers.

The following two cases will be considered: (a) where readers have priority over writers, and (b) where writers have priority over readers.

This problem is fairly typical. For example, compare it with an airline reservation system where many enquiries on a central database are allowed, but only one travel agent/booking office at a time can be allowed to change the database and reserve a seat.

10.7.1 Readers have priority

Exclusive access to write to the file can be achieved by using a single semaphore w, as described earlier.

Writing

wait (w)

  exclusive access to alter the file.

signal (w)

Reading

A variable readcount (initially 0) is needed to note how many processes are currently reading the file. The first reader sets the w semaphore to stop any writers, and the last reader clears the w semaphore.

wait (x)
  readcount := readcount + 1
  IF readcount = 1 THEN wait (w)
signal (x)

  read the file.

wait (x)
  readcount := readcount − 1
  IF readcount = 0 THEN signal (w)
signal (x)

Note that as the variable readcount is accessed by all readers concurrently, it must be 'protected' by including it in a critical region which is controlled by semaphore x.

So long as there is at least one process reading the file, any other readers can also access the file concurrently (although they must pass one at a time through the critical region protected by x).

If a process is writing to the file, the first reader will halt on semaphore w, and all other readers on semaphore x.

10.7.2 *Writers have priority*

In many respects the solution is the converse of the previous solution, in that:

(1) A semaphore r is needed to inhibit all readers while the writers are wanting to access the file.
(2) A variable writecount is needed to control the setting of r.
(3) A semaphore y is needed to control access to writecount.
(4) A semaphore w is *still* needed to achieve exclusive write access to the file.

This leads to the following sequence:

Writing

```
wait (y)
    writecount := writecount + 1
    IF writecount = 1 THEN wait (r)        {Stop Readers}
signal (y)

wait (w)
    write to the file                      {With exclusive access}
signal (w)

wait (y)
    writecount := writecount − 1
    IF writecount = 0 THEN signal (r)      {Free Readers}
signal (y)
```

Reading

(1) Multiple reading must still be allowed, and so the variable readcount is still needed.
(2) The r semaphore must be set *before* the w semaphore is set. If w is set after, a *deadlock* situation could result (with a writer holding r and waiting for w, a reader holding w and waiting for r).
(3) There must be a signal on the r semaphore before the reading sequence, as multiple reading is allowed.

(4) A queue of readers must not be allowed to build up on r. In principle, the order in which processes are freed on a signal is undefined, and so a writer waiting on r could be overtaken indefinitely by readers which arrived later. By introducing an additional semaphore z immediately before the wait on r, a reader executing its preamble code and signalling on r can only have a writer waiting to be freed.

Consequently, the sequence for reading from the file now appears as follows:

```
wait (z)
    wait (r)
        wait (x)
            readcount := readcount + 1
            IF readcount = 1 THEN wait (w)
        signal (x)
    signal (r)
signal (z)

    read the file

wait (x)
    readcount := readcount - 1
    IF readcount = 0 THEN signal (w)
signal (x)
```

State of the queues

Readers only in the system	Writers only in the system
w set No queues	w and r set Writers queue on w

Both readers and writers with read first	Both readers and writers with write first
w set by reader r set by writer All writers queue on w 1 reader queues on r Other readers queue on z	w set by writer r set by writer Writers queue on w 1 reader queues on r Other readers queue on z

10.8   Summary

This chapter has examined the problems associated with cooperating processes which may need to synchronise their actions or are competing for access to a shared resource, such as a shared data structure. The notion of a 'critical region of code' has been introduced, so process competition can be avoided by making the region mutually exclusive. The difficulties of using a flag to identify such a region have been discussed, and the semaphore operations of initialisation, wait and signal have been described, as a more convenient primitive.

Possible implementations of the semaphore operations have been presented, both in the context of multiprogramming and of multiprocessor systems. In addition to the simple examples of using semaphores to implement mutual exclusion and process synchronisation in a producer-consumer situation, a more comprehensive example, addressing the classical reader's and writer's problem, has been presented.

10.9   References and bibliography

E.W. Dijkstra (1968a). 'Cooperating Sequential Processes', *Programming Languages,* (ed. F. Genuys), Academic Press, New York.

E.W. Dijkstra (1968b). 'The Structure of the THE Multiprogramming System', *Communications of the ACM*, Vol. 11, pp. 341-6.

E.W. Dijkstra (1965). 'Solution of a Problem in Concurrent Programming Control', *Communications of the ACM*, Vol. 8, p. 569.

L. Lamport (1968). 'The Mutual Exclusion Problem: Part I - A Theory of Interprocess Communication', *Journal of the ACM*, Vol. 33, No. 2, pp. 313-26.

L. Lamport (1968). 'The Mutual Exclusion Problem: Part II - Statement and Solutions', *Journal of the ACM*, Vol. 33, No. 2, pp. 327-48.

M. Raynal (1986). *Algorithms for Mutual Exclusion*, MIT Press, Cambridge, Mass.

11 Process Synchronisation - Language-Based Approaches

11.1 Introduction

It has been shown how semaphores can be used for process communication and to achieve mutual exclusion. They can, of course, be used also for more complicated synchronisation problems. The main advantage of semaphores over more *ad hoc* methods is that the semaphore invariant provides a means of treating synchronisation problems with mathematical rigour. It can actually be proved, rather than just assumed, that the solutions are correct.

The main problem with semaphores is that, for large and complex systems, they leave considerable scope for programming errors, and it is still quite easy to program systems containing time-dependent errors. There has therefore been considerable research into alternative techniques for constructing operating systems with reduced opportunities for such errors. Two main approaches can be distinguished, which can be characterised as (a) language based, and (b) message based. These approaches will be discussed in this and the subsequent chapter.

The language-based approach to operating system design (and indeed other forms of concurrent programming) aims to facilitate production of correct systems by use of programming languages whose semantics have been defined in such a way that it is possible to detect potential time-dependencies by semantic checks in the compiler. Thus, a program that compiles without errors cannot exhibit any time-dependencies (though its synchronisation may still not be correct!).

There have been many different attempts in this general direction. One of the earliest to meet with success was introduced by Brinch-Hansen, and subsequently developed by Hoare (Hoare, 1974) in the form of Monitors. The monitor concept is used within the programming language Modula-2 to provide an appropriate synchronisation mechanism. In addition to process synchronisation, modern languages designed for the production of real-time and embedded system software generally have mechanisms within the language to provide support for the systems programmer. The facilities of Modula-2, Ada and occam will be surveyed within this chapter.

157

11.2   Monitors

In monitors, two related concepts are combined, namely *system modularity*, and *synchronisation*. The form of modularity encouraged by monitors affords inter-module protection through static checks in the compiler. Thus, monitors can be said to have both synchronisation and protection implications.

The approach taken to modularity is relevant to ordinary sequential programs as well as operating systems. The idea is that, when a structure is defined, the operations that can be performed on it should be defined at the same time, and the language semantics should prevent any other operations from being performed on it. As a simple (sequential) example, consider defining a stack data structure in Pascal. The definitions might be:

```
TYPE stack = RECORD
     st: ARRAY [1..maxstack] OF integer;
     sp: 1..maxstack
     END
```

The push and pop operations are then defined as:

```
PROCEDURE push (VAR s: stack; item: integer);
     BEGIN
     s.st[s.sp] := item;
     s.sp := s.sp + 1
     END;

PROCEDURE pop (VAR s: stack; VAR item: integer);
     BEGIN
     s.sp := s.sp - 1;
     item := s.st[s.sp]
     END
```

This is a perfectly good implementation of a stack but it leaves open the possibility to 'cheat' by accessing s.st or s.sp directly rather than via the push and pop procedures. For example, an instruction to discard five items from the top of the stack might be written as

```
s.sp := s.sp - 5
```

However, this knowledge of the stack structure precludes the ability to change the organisation of the stack, say to linked lists rather than arrays.

11.2.1 Encapsulation

A monitor *encapsulates* the definition of a data structure and the operations on it in such a way that the components of the structure can be accessed only from within the procedures that define operations on it. For example:

```
MONITOR stack;

  CONST maxstack = 100;
  VAR st: ARRAY [1..maxstack] OF integer
  sp: 1..maxstack;

  PROCEDURE push (item: integer);
    BEGIN
      st[sp] := item;
      sp := sp + 1
    END;

  PROCEDURE pop (VAR item: integer);
    BEGIN
      sp := sp - 1;
      item := st[sp]
    END;

  BEGIN
    sp := 1            {initialisation code}
  END;
```

This defines a new data type *stack*, so the variables can be declared in the usual way:

```
  VAR s1, s2: stack;
```

However, the components of S1 and S2 cannot be accessed; all that can be done is to call the push and pop procedures. The notation for doing this is similar to the notation for accessing components of record structures:

```
  s1.push (item)
  s2.pop  (item)
```

Note that the monitor body defines the initialisation to be performed automatically on the data structures when it is declared.

For sequential programming the main advantage of this kind of structure lies in the enforcement of 'clean' programming techniques and the consequential improvement in maintainability of the software. Also, if program-proving techniques are ever to be useful, this kind of structuring seems essential - it enables a verification to be made that all uses of all stacks in a program are correct and only requires a check on a very small sequence of code.

11.2.2　Mutual exclusion

The first requirement with shared data structures is to provide mutual exclusion on accesses to them. With monitors this is easy. First the procedures of a monitor are mutually exclusive; that is, only one process at a time may be executing code within a given monitor. The compiler can implement this by associating a mutual exclusion semaphore with each monitor-type object declared. The semaphore is WAITED at the start and SIGNALLED at the end of each monitor call. An alternative for multiprogrammed systems that do not have fast crisis time devices is to inhibit interrupts throughout execution of monitor procedures.

Given this rule, and assuming that the language also has a means of defining processes, determinate operation can be guaranteed by the simple semantic rule: 'Processes may not share any data that is not accessed through a monitor'.

11.2.3　Communication

Mutual exclusion is only one part of the synchronisation problem. It is also necessary to provide the means whereby processes wait for something to happen, and are woken when it does. Many different mechanisms for this have been proposed, but two extremes are:

(1) High-level approach.

Since the waiting will be dependent on a shared data structure (for example, CHAR_COUNT = 0), a statement

AWAIT <Boolean expression>

can be introduced that can be used only within monitor procedures. The procedures delay the process until the Boolean expression - which represents a relation on the monitor's data structure - is true. No explicit wake-up operation is needed and any change to the data structure may implicitly wake a halted process.

(2) Low-level approach.

The alternative approach requires monitor procedures to synchronise explicitly using semaphores or a related mechanism. Obviously this will be rather less convenient but may be more efficient.

11.3 Modula-2

Finally in this chapter, a number of languages will be discussed, with reference to the synchronisation facilities provided within then. The language Modula-2 was designed in 1978 by Niklaus Wirth, and is intended for the construction of system software on minicomputers. This language is based on Pascal, but has a number of interesting features that distinguish it from most other operating system languages. In particular:

(1) *MODULES*

As the name of the language implies, it is intended for the production of modular systems. To this end it includes a construct called a MODULE, which achieves the 'encapsulation' effect of monitors in a somewhat different way.

(2) *PROCESSES*

The language is designed primarily for writing multiprogramming systems for single-processor configurations. It therefore offers only very basic facilities for multiprogramming, which are firmly based on the concept of the coroutine. As a consequence, there is no built-in scheduling strategy; the system programmer is in full control.

(3) *DEVICES AND INTERRUPTS*

The language includes facilities for handling devices directly at the interrupt level. These are based on the PDP11 device driving and interrupt systems, but the principles could be extended to match other machines.

11.3.1 Modules

The module construct in Modula-2 is designed to provide the 'encapsulation' of data and operations that were discussed in connection with monitors, but without the synchronisation implications. The form of a module declaration is:

MODULE module-name;

FROM other-module-name IMPORT identifier-list;
FROM yet-another-module-name IMPORT identifier-list;

...

EXPORT identifier-list;

block of code

Names from outside the module can be used only if they are mentioned in the IMPORT section, and the EXPORT section specifies names that can be used by other modules (provided that they IMPORT them). The notion of exports in Modula-2 is more general than in monitors, as (a) the list of names to be exported is specified rather than exporting all procedure names, and (b) names other than those of procedures can be exported. This latter facility is particularly useful for exporting:

    (1) Constants and read-only variables (though Modula-2 does not include any way of specifying that an exported variable is read-only).

    (2) Type identifiers, without necessarily exporting any information about the structure of the type.

It is recommended, but not mandatory, that shared variables (that is, variables shared between 'concurrent' activities) should be isolated within modules, which are then called interface modules.

11.3.2 Processes - coroutines

Coroutines are processes that are executed by a single processor one at a time. Transfers from one process to another are programmed explicitly.

Modula-2 implements coroutines with a built-in type called PROCESS. This is in fact a structure used to keep the set of information, such as a register dump, needed to restart the process. However, the programmer is not able to access the contents of a PROCESS variable explicitly - the type PROCESS and the procedures that operate on variables of this type must be imported from a built-in module SYSTEM. A new process is initiated by declaring a variable of type process and then initialising it using the procedure NEWPROCESS

    VAR p: process;
    ...
    newprocess (code, base, size, p);

where code is the name of a procedure that specifies the actions of the new process, base and size are the address and size of the workspace to be used by this process and the variable p will subsequently be used to identify this process. A transfer of control between two processes is then achieved by calling

    transfer (p1,p2)

where p1 and p2 are both process variables. The effect is to:

    (1) Suspend the current process and save its restart information in variable p1.
    (2) Enter the process designated by p2.

11.3.3 Devices and interrupts

Actual control of devices is handled by allowing the programmer to specify the addresses of operands, thus mapping them on to the hardware control registers, for example,

VAR diskcr [177460B]: SET OF 0..15

This in itself is not a great breakthrough, but it is the method of handling interrupts that is of interest. After writing to the device control register to enable interrupts, the procedure

iotransfer (p1,p2,va)

is called, where p1 and p2 are variables of type PROCESS and va is the address of the interrupt vector for the device. The effect is similar to transfer (p1,p2) except that a return to p1 is prepared for later. When the interrupt actually occurs, a transfer (p2,p1) is executed automatically to bring control back to the device driver.

Obviously some masking of interrupts is needed; this is achieved by permitting each module to indicate the processor priority at which it should be run.

11.4 Ada

Ada as a programming language has been developed to meet many of the needs that arise in programming embedded systems which have a long life-cycle and hence have a high demand on maintainability. Embedded systems typically consist of a number of closely cooperating parallel processes, or tasks as they are referred to in Ada. Much of the syntax of Ada is similar to that of Modula-2, and whilst it has many features that could be described and discussed, it is the areas that relate to the support of concurrent processes and inter-process communication that will be considered in this text.

Ada supports modular programs and multi-tasking. Its support of separate module compilation allows compile-time checking of type compatibility across module boundaries. This is achieved by the use of the *package* and *task* constructs. Ada can also be regarded as a systems implementation language since there are also facilities for interrupt vectoring and interfacing with machine-language modules by way of machine-specific libraries which can be combined with other modules.

In Ada, packages are generally defined in two parts - the package specification and the package body. The specification identifies the facilities that the package supplies and the body implements these facilities. Packages are a mechanism for *information hiding* and *data encapsulation*, and can be used to group logically related entities, such as constants, types and sub-programs. Exported data may take with it assignment and relation operations. The packages are generic with the final details of their specification given by parameters.

There is separate compilation of all significant program parts including specification parts (i.e. interface definitions) separately from implementation parts (bodies of program units). There is also delayed, separate compilation of details of procedures; at the normal point of declaration is a program stub. This provides good language support for stepwise refinement.

The other type of module in Ada is the task. Like packages, tasks in Ada consist of two parts; a specification and a body. They may be activated at any time, and they can safely die naturally or be aborted. Tasks have entries which may be called by other tasks, and this allows two tasks to communicate or synchronise.

11.4.1   Rendezvous

Process synchronisation and mutual exclusion are provided by the same mechanism, namely that of *rendezvous*. A rendezvous is a point of full synchronisation between two tasks. Whichever task reaches the rendezvous point first waits for the other. At the rendezvous, data may be exchanged in either or both directions, a special section of code may be executed and then the tasks continue their execution in parallel.

In Ada the two tasks are distinguished by which contains the special section of code that is executed while the two tasks are together; this is called the *accept* statement. If the section of code only contains non-executable statements then the task achieves only synchronisation. In order for other processes to rendezvous with this task, the owner of the accept statement gives it a unique name that is made public by placing a corresponding *entry* statement in the public declaration part of that process. The other task contains an entry statement which is identical to a procedure call statement.

This mechanism readily satisfies synchronisation and mutual exclusion is provided by the special section of executable code within the accept statement. However, since mutual exclusion requires synchronisation at the same time there is a need to define intermediate tasks with the sole job of always, or invariably, being ready for the rendezvous, which is in contrast to the basis of message passing systems.

Consider the following outline program in Ada:

```
task A is                              task B is
   {public part of A}                     {public part of B}
   ..                                      ..
   ..                                      entry C;
   ..                                      ..
end A;                                  end B;

task body A is                         task body B is
   {private part of A}                    {private part of B}
   ..                                      ..
   B.C; {call entry in B}              accept C;
   ..                                      ..
end A;                                  end B;
```

Since task *B* contains the accept statement then it provides the corresponding entry in the public part of the task. The task *A* expresses its requirement to rendezvous with task *B* by its call *B.C*. This states both the identifier name and it is prefixed by *B.* to show the task that *C* is associated with, thereby avoiding ambiguities if the identifier is used in other task declarations. So far as task *A* is concerned, *C* is an external reference, and therefore the specification of *B* must be available when the body of *A* is compiled.

The operation of the rendezvous in this case proceeds as follows. Two options exist, dependent on whether task *A* arrives first or task *B* is waiting to have its accept matched by another task. If task *A* arrives first, then it is suspended and placed in a queue of tasks which are associated with the accept statement in task *B*. If task *B* executes its accept before there is a call from task *A*, then task *B* is suspended at that point waiting an execution of the *B.C* call. Once both of the parties arrive, then the rendezvous takes place.

Giving a further example, the following sequence illustrates how a semaphore might be implemented in Ada:

```
task type semaphore is
   entry wait;
   entry signal;
end semaphore

task body semaphore is
   begin
   loop
      accept wait;
      accept signal;
   end loop;
   end semaphore;
```

A semaphore would be declared using a task declaration of type semaphore, such as

    s:semaphore;

and its use, for example to provide mutual exclusion on shared data, would be by the sequence

    s.wait;
        access shared data
    s.signal;

Several tasks can issue calls to the same entry of another task, and these entry calls are put in a queue associated with the entry. They will be accepted in a first-in-first-out (FIFO) order. It can be seen that whilst the calling task must name the task that it is calling explicitly, the called task does not have any way of specifying with which task it will rendezvous. This defines two classes of tasks, *active* and *passive,* where active tasks call upon the services of passive tasks, and the passive tasks provide the services by the provision of suitable entry points.

The inclusion of a *select* statement in Ada allows the passive task to scan the task wait queues in search of an active-task descriptor. There are three types of select statement; the *selective wait*, the *conditional entry call*, and the *timed entry call*. The selective wait statement allows a task to accept entry calls from more than one task in a deterministic fashion. The conditional entry call is a non-blocking entry call, where the calling task does not wait if the called task is not ready. It is therefore free to proceed with other work. The timed entry call is very similar, except that the calling task specifies a period of time for the called task to accept the entry call, before it 'gives up' and proceeds with other work.

The full implementation of the select statement is beyond the scope of this book as it is a very powerful statement with non-trivial semantics. The following example, however, illustrates the use of a selective wait in a producer-consumer situation.

```
task body consumer is
    A: character;
begin
    loop
        select
            accept receive (C: in character) do
                A := C;
            end receive;
            put (upper (A));
```

        or
                terminate;
            end select;
        end loop;
    end consumer

The consumer now terminates by selection of the *terminate* only after it has determined that the producer has terminated.

11.5 occam

The discussion about Ada has been concerned only with its handling of process synchronisation and mutual exclusion by the use of the rendezvous. It is a complex programming language which supports extensive data types and a substantial number of syntactic structures. In contrast the language occam, Jones (1988), Inmos (1988), appears relatively simple. One of the major conceptual difference between Ada and occam is that in occam, data may not be shared between tasks. Occam is fundamentally a distributed processing language, where data is communicated between processes only by explicitly sending a message from one process to another by way of named channels. Both are capable of providing support for communicating processes, such as the CSP techniques described by Hoare (1978).

11.5.1 Processes and channels

In occam, programs are built up from processes. Each process may be regarded as a 'black box' with some particular internal state. The processes are finite, such that each process starts, performs a number of actions and then terminates. The simplest process is an action, and an action can consist of an assignment, input or output. Processes may be combined together to form programs by way of process constructors. Since each process may itself consist of other processes, some of which may execute in parallel, the concept of processes as used in occam means that there is an amount of internal concurrency in the language. The degree of concurrency which is achieved at any given time will alter as processes start and terminate.

As an extension to the determinism of languages such as Pascal and to allow for alternatives and repetitions which are non-deterministic, occam uses the concept of a *guard*ed construct. This means that, given several choices, one is selected at random. In a guarded construct, the guard may be a Boolean expression which is followed by a list of statements which may only be executed if the guard is **TRUE**. So, for example

```
[    guard1 > command1
[ ]  guard2 > command2
[ ]  guard3 > command3
[ ]  ...etc
]
```

where guard*n* is a Boolean expression and command*n* is a list of statements, would mean that the sequence

```
[    x >= y → m := x
[ ]  y >= x → m := y
]
```

would assign the larger of the two variables x or y to the third variable m, as if one guard is TRUE, that is selected; if both guards are TRUE then either may be chosen at random. In the general case, if neither guard is true then the process aborts.

In occam, the three basic constructors are those of SEQ, PAR and ALT. The SEQ constructor specifies that the following processes are performed in a sequential manner, so that for example

```
SEQ
    process1
    process2
```

means that process1 is executed first, followed on its completion by process2.

To provide concurrency, the constructor PAR means that processes are executed in parallel. For example,

```
PAR
    process1
    process2
```

means that process1 and process2 execute in parallel with each other.

In occam, the level of indentation following the constructor is an inherent part of the language. Successive indents are of two spaces, and provide the function of a guard.

The third constructor, the ALT or alternative, provides a level of selection between processes. The ALT construct takes the list of processes within its guard and performs the first process that it finds to satisfy its appropriate guard. An example which illustrates the use of the ALT construct is as follows:

```
ALT
    flag & c.1 ? input
        c.3 ! input
    flag & c.2 ? input
        c.3 ! input
    NOT flag & c.1 ? input
        c.3 ! input
```

where ? specifies an input operation and ! an output operation.

This process will look for input on two channels c.1 and c.2. While flag is TRUE, then input on either c.1 or c.2 will be read and passed on unchanged down channel c.3, the selection of either c.1 or c.2 being taken at random. However when flag is FALSE, c.2 will be ignored and only c.1 will be passed on. It is important that one of the guards must be TRUE, otherwise if all the guards are FALSE then the ALT statement behaves as a STOP and the program becomes deadlocked.

A number of other constructors exist within the language, for example to provide priorities and replication of these constructors. For example, the use of the replication of the SEQ construct expressed as

SEQ $i = 0$ for 5

provides replication of those statements within the guard of this SEQ to be repeated for values of i from 0 to 4. Similar replication constructs exist for the PAR and ALT constructs.

Any pair of processes communicate with each other using a one-way point-to-point channel called an occam channel which connects the two processes. One of the processes outputs a message to the channel and the other inputs the message from the same channel. The important point is that with these channels the communications are synchronised and unbuffered. When a channel is used to connect two processes then communication between the processes can only take place when both input and output processes are ready. Whichever process reaches its input or output statement must wait until the other process is ready. Once both processes are ready then the inputting and outputting can proceed. This form of communication is equivalent to hand-shaking in hardware systems.

A process may be ready to communicate on any one of a number of channels. Communication takes place when another process is ready to communicate on one of the channels. Since a process may have internal concurrency, it may have many input channels and output channels performing communications at the same time.

11.5.2   Inter-process communication

We have already discussed in the previous section that occam provides inter-process communications by means of channels. These channels provide point-to-point communications which ensure that messages are both synchronised and unbuffered. Hence the requirements of synchronisation of processes is ensured within the language. We can illustrate such synchronisation in the example of a simple queue. The program considers data as flowing down a series of slots, where the slots form an array of parallel processors which pass data between the slots. A simple approach to this might contain the following:

```
[20] CHAN OF INT slot:
PAR i := 0 FOR 19
    WHILE TRUE
        INT y:
        SEQ
            slot[i] ? y
            slot[i+1] ! y
```

In this case we define an array of 20 slots, and use a replicated PAR construct so that 19 parallel processes are set up which continually transfer data between adjacent slots in the queue. The synchronisation between successive slots is achieved by the SEQ construct. However, it should be noted that this represents only a fragment of a program; it does not provide a mechanism for input into slot[0] or indeed any effective output for data from slot[20].

11.6   Summary

The difficulty of using the semaphore mechanism described in chapter 10 has led to alternative, higher level mechanisms for providing process synchronisation. Modern high-level languages designed for systems programming now incorporate constructs for supporting process creation, communication and synchronisation. This chapter has briefly examined the mechanisms within three such languages; Modula-2, Ada and occam.

Initially the chapter examined the concept of a Monitor, being a means of supporting modularity and also encapsulating data structures with associated access procedures. The provision of mutual exclusion within the monitor code is inherent within the mechanism. An equivalent mechanism is described in the context of Modula-2 via its Module construct. The language also provides other support for systems programming, including a device handling capability and multiprogramming facilities via a coroutine mechanism.

The Ada programming language also provides mechanisms for encapsulation and multi-tasking through its package and task constructs. The main form of synchronisation is implemented through a rendezvous mechanism. This also allows data to be exchanged between processes when they synchronise, through the execution of a sequence of code within an accept statement.

The occam language is designed to be more simple than Ada, and this is very apparent in the mechanisms provided for expressing parallelism. Inter-process communication takes place via channels, which provide point-to-point communication between processes. They can be used for synchronisation or data transfer, and are equally applicable to multiprocessor or single processor configurations.

11.7 References and bibliography

P. Brinch-Hansen (1976). 'The Solo Operating System in Processes, Monitors and Classes', *Software Practice and Experience*, Vol. 6, pp. 165-200.

G.R. Brookes and A.J. Stewart (1989). *Introduction to occam 2 on the Transputer*, Macmillan, London.

N.H. Gehani (1983). *Ada   An Advanced Introduction*, Prentice Hall, Englewood Cliffs NJ.

A.N. Habermann and D.E. Perry (1983). *Ada for Experienced Programmers*, Addison-Wesley, Reading, Mass.

C.A.R. Hoare (1974). 'Monitors; An Operating System Structuring Concept', *Communications of the ACM*, Vol. 17, pp. 549-57.

C.A.R. Hoare (1978). 'Communicating Sequential Processes', *Communications of the ACM*, Vol. 21, pp. 666-77.

Inmos (1988). *Occam Reference Manual*, Prentice Hall, London.

J. Jones and N. Goldsmith (1988). *Programming in Occam 2*, Prentice Hall, London.

A.M. Lister and K.J. Maynard (1976). 'An Implementation of Monitors', *Software Practice and Experience*, Vol. 6, pp. 377-86.

I.C. Pyle (1985). *The Ada Programming Language*, Prentice Hall, London.

H.A. Schmid (1976). 'On the Efficient Implementation of Conditional Critical Regions and the Construction of Monitors', *Acta Informatica*, Vol. 6, No. 3, pp. 227-79.

N. Wirth (1977). 'MODULA: A Language for Modular Programming', *Software Practice and Experience*, Vol. 7, pp. 3-36.

12 Process Synchronisation - Message-Based Approaches

12.1 Introduction

The major problem when using mechanisms such as semaphores, as described in chapter 10, is that the primitive nature of a semaphore leaves considerable scope for errors in synchronisation and the potential for deadlocks. An alternative approach is that provided by message-based systems, which try to provide operations more closely suited to the needs of developing operating system modules. The synchronisation is performed 'behind the scenes' by higher level mechanisms, which are not susceptible to time dependencies.

One feature of the message-based approaches is that they are equally applicable to distributed systems, where processor interactions may take place across a telecommunications network, and to uni-processor or tightly coupled systems, where shared memory is accessible to the processes and processors.

The message-based approaches are complementary to the language-based approaches in that they may be used by the language support systems in implementing the facilities within the programming languages. Being language independent, they also provide more flexibility when developing system software in a mixed language environment, providing primitive operations for enhancing the basic language facilities.

Message systems were devised in an attempt to realise two important objectives in operating systems design. These are:

(1) Determinacy - the system's behaviour should not be timing-dependent. This has already been discussed at some length.

(2) Protection - because operating systems need to be altered frequently, and because these alterations may introduce errors, it is desirable to protect the individual modules of the system against the effects of errors in other modules so that an error in a relatively unimportant module does not crash the entire system.

The main problem with protecting modules from one another is that they need to share variables, and a fairly sophisticated protection system is required

172

if they are to be allowed to share *only* certain variables. Furthermore, a module can quite easily destroy the operation of another by interfering with those variables that are shared.

The problem with determinacy, on the other hand, is that when synchronisation requirements become complex, their programming becomes quite difficult. It should be noted too that synchronisation arises *only* when processes share resources. If this sharing could be eliminated, then both the protection and the determinacy problems could be solved.

Processes that form part of an operating system cannot run in a vacuum - they have to communicate with one another. It is this need for communication that mainly results in processes sharing data. So, one approach in designing an operating system is to keep the processes separate - that is, not to allow them to share anything - and then provide them with an alternative means of communication by passing *messages* to one another.

If this approach is adopted, then operating system modules can be protected from one another using the same mechanisms that isolate and protect user jobs from one another (for example, memory segmentation). Clearly the message-passing module is an exception in that it is the only part of the system that needs explicitly to access shared data, and the only one that performs explicit synchronisation. Other modules synchronise indirectly via the message operations.

12.2 Message-passing operations

Clearly the minimum set of operations needed are those to *send* and to *receive* messages. The receive operation will halt the process until a message is actually received; the send will free the destination process if it is waiting for a message.

Assuming a minimal system of this type, there are two ways in which it might be implemented. In the first the two processes are very closely synchronised. The destination process must be waiting for a message before the sender sends it (alternatively, the sender is halted if this is not so). This tight synchronisation, similar to the Ada rendezvous or occam channel, has the advantage of not requiring messages to be buffered but it implies a degree of synchronisation between communicating processes which might not be desirable.

If processes are to be permitted to operate asynchronously, some form of buffering is required in the message system. If each process has associated with it a queue of messages not yet read (p.queue) and a semaphore controls this queue (p.sem), then the message operations can be implemented as:

send (message, dest)

wait (mbuf)	Wait for message buffer available
wait (mutex)	Mutual exclusion on message queue
acquire free buffer	
copy message to buffer	
link buffer to dest.queue	
signal (dest.sem)	Wake destination process
signal (mutex)	Release mutual exclusion

receive (message)

wait (own.sem)	Wait for a message to arrive
wait (mutex)	Mutual exclusion on message queue
unlink buffer from own.queue	
copy buffer to message	
add buffer to freelist	
signal (mbuf)	Indicate another message buffer freed
signal (mutex)	Release mutual exclusion

where *mbuf* is initialised to the total number of message buffers available in the system, and *own* and *dest* refer to a single semaphore for each process, which is the queue of messages for that process (initially zero).

There are three points worth noting about this system:

(1) Observe that it is vital to keep the two waits in the *send* and *receive* operations in the order specified. Reversing them could lead to deadlocks.

(2) The solution above involves a deadlock danger if all message buffers are used up and no process can continue without first sending a message. This is especially serious if user jobs are allowed to use the message operations.

(3) Note the similarity between the above and the producer/consumer situation given earlier. Logically the two cases are the same.

The message-passing scheme that has been described is structured in such a way that all message traffic takes the form of a message request from a source to a destination which is followed by a reply message from the original destination to the original source. If we regard this from the source point of view, the operation is similar to that involved in calling a procedure and then waiting for the procedure to finish, since in both perspectives, the caller provides some parameters, starts the operation, waits until the operation is complete and then gets some result values.

In some distributed operating systems (Birrell and Nelson, 1984) the inter-process communication is achieved by the use of the *remote procedure call*. For example, if a source process wants to read a block from a remote file, it calls a procedure known as a stub procedure running on the same machine, using a standard procedure call instruction. The stub procedure sends a request message to the file server and waits for a reply. On the destination machine, the message is accepted by another stub procedure, which calls the ultimate destination using a standard procedure call instruction. Results are returned to the source process in a similar way, with 'called' procedures passing results to the caller, and the two stub procedures communicating via messages.

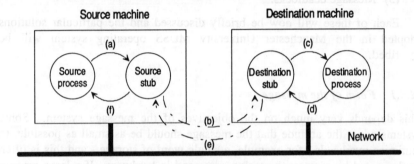

Figure 12.1   Remote procedure calls

In this style of operation, neither the source nor destination need be aware that messages are being used; they only see calls to local procedures. It is only the respective stubs that are aware of the messages. The operation of this sequence is shown in figure 12.1, where the various stages are:

(a) and (c)   Procedure calls
(b) and (e)   Messages
(d) and (f)   Procedure returns

This form of inter-process communication has a number of potential disadvantages. The passing of parameters is achieved by reference rather than the more simple case of passing by value. If the source and destination machines have different representations for information, as for example, in representing integers or floating point numbers, then considerable overheads will be incurred performing the conversions into a standard network format. In addition, other difficulties may arise in the use of remote procedure calls, such as if the destination process faults when executing a remote call, so that recovery from the failure must be performed.

12.3 Practical considerations

While in principle the send and receive facilities described are sufficient for a simple message system, in practice there are some further considerations which tend to make actual systems more complex. Some of the most important of these are:

(1) Form of the message.
(2) Addressing of processes.
(3) Type of message queuing discipline.
(4) Message validation/protection.
(5) Message deadlocks.

Each of these will now be briefly discussed and the particular solutions adopted in the Manchester University MUSS operating system will be described.

12.3.1 Form of the message

This depends very much on the objectives of the message system. Some systems adopt the attitude that the message should be as small as possible, to minimise overheads - for example, a single word of storage - and this is often implemented by a message-passing command in hardware. If a large amount of data is to be passed, the data can be placed in a file and the message then contains the file name. This leads to significant overheads in the case where intermediate amounts of information are to be passed, which rather invalidates the reason for making the messages short in the first place.

MUSS is a partly message-based system. Certain key parts of the system communicate and synchronise directly, but the higher-level modules communicate via messages and are completely protected from one another. Here the approach adopted is to allow messages to have arbitrary size (within reason). This is achieved by defining a message to be a segment of virtual store. It can then be passed efficiently by transferring a pointer from the sender's to the receiver's segment table.

Using this mechanism, complete input/output documents can be passed around the system as messages. For example, an input spooler simply reads characters into a segment (which looks like a large array of memory!) and when a terminator is recognised, the whole segment is sent as a message to its destination.

In fact, a small amount of control information (about 100 bytes) is passed along with every message. This is used to indicate to the destination process what is to be done with the segment (for example, print it, file it). In cases where this short header is sufficient, the segment can be omitted entirely, and this option is often used for internal control messages and for interactive input/output.

12.3.2 Addressing of processes

Clearly it is necessary to have a way of specifying to the send message operation *which* process is to receive the message. This in itself presents no difficulties - each process can be assigned a unique name and this can be used for identification purposes. (There is, however, a problem of identifying processes in other machines in a multi-computer system.)

The main question that arises is: 'How do processes specify with whom they wish to communicate?'. In MUSS there are three possible techniques and these represent three different ways of using the message system.

(1) The destination process name is built in when the module is programmed. For example, processes communicating with the file manager will use a standard name for it.

(2) The destination process is specified at run-time, say by users' job control statements. This applies to processes such as output spoolers; the user can select which device the output goes to by specifying the destination process name. Device controllers are given standard names such as LPT, LASER, etc.

(3) The message might be a reply to a process from which a message has just been received. For this purpose (but see also section 12.3.4 below) each message includes the identity of the sender to allow replies to be sent easily. This is useful for internal system messages (for example, *Request Message* - 'Get me a file please' - *Reply Message* - 'Here it is') and also for interactive jobs, whose output is directed to the same terminal from which input was last received.

12.3.3 Type of message queuing discipline

Obviously the simplest is a straightforward first-in-first-out queue, but this may not be satisfactory if some messages are more urgent than others. Alternatives may include specifying message priorities so that they can automatically be queued in some priority order, or allowing the destination process to inspect its message queue and select which message to read.

MUSS gives each process eight separate message queues (called channels) and the sender can choose to which channel a message is to be sent. The destination can then establish conventions as to the use of each channel, and may choose from which channel the next message is to be read. Thus, for example, an output spooler may reserve one channel for normal documents, one for high-priority documents and one for operator requests, such as to abandon printing the current document or to restart printing it again.

12.3.4   Message validation / protection

A process may wish to restrict the set of processes from which messages will be accepted. One essential step to achieve this is for the system to supply, with each message, enough information about the sender (for example, process identifier, user identifier) to allow the receiver to validate the message. In addition to this, MUSS allows a process to set each of its message channels into one of three states:

OPEN   - messages accepted from all sources
CLOSED   - messages accepted from no sources
DEDICATED   - messages accepted from a specified source

The message system automatically rejects messages that do not fall into an acceptable category. In addition, a process can specify that a channel is to be closed after one message has been accepted, thus protecting itself against a shower of messages being sent by some faulty process to which the channel is temporarily open.

12.3.5   Message deadlocks

Finally the question arises 'What if a process is waiting for a message that never comes?'. Of course, this means some part of the system is misbehaving, but one of the objectives is to enable each module to protect itself against errors in others. This is particularly important in a system like MUSS, where user jobs as well as system modules can send and receive messages. The solution adopted here is to specify a time limit when waiting for messages. If this is exceeded, the waiting process wakes up and is informed that no message exists. This is a useful mechanism, as it allows each process to effect some sensible recovery action if a process with which it is communicating fails to answer. It also has other uses - for example, timing out a job if the user fails to type anything for a long time.

12.4   Solution of the reader's and writer's problem using messages

The easiest way of using a message system to solve the reader's and writer's problem is to have a process in control of the database, so that the other processes wishing to access the information in the files must send messages to the controlling process. In an ultra-secure system, the controlling process might be the only one allowed to access the file. The other processes then either request records from the controlling process or send records to be incorporated into the database. Although this is very secure and 'clean', as only one process ever accesses the files, it incurs a number of overheads, particularly as the controlling process is unable to service multiple read requests in parallel (as requested in the problem specification).

The most satisfactory solution is therefore for the controlling process to grant permission to access the file and to leave the actual file access to the individual processes. The sequences within the reading and writing processes might therefore be:

In reading process	*In writing process*
Send message asking for permission to read the file	Send message asking for permission to write to the file
Wait for a reply to say 'ok'	Wait for a reply to say 'ok'
READ THE FILE	WRITE TO THE FILE
Send message to say 'I have finished'	Send message to say 'I have finished'

No priority decisions are included within the reading and writing processes. All such decisions have to be made by the controlling process.

12.4.1 Design of the controlling process

The controlling process has to service three types of message, namely requests to read, requests to write and the 'I have finished' messages. It is far easier to organise the controlling process if these can be serviced independently, and so a separate channel might be dedicated for each type of message, namely:

Channel 1 - Finished messages
Channel 2 - Write requests
Channel 3 - Read requests

The order of servicing the channels therefore has a bearing on the relative priorities of the readers and writers.

The following algorithm is one possible way of organising the controlling process so that writers have priority (recall that this case was quite complex when implemented using semaphores). In addition to servicing write request messages before read request messages in order to achieve the necessary priority, a means of achieving mutual exclusion for the writers must be provided. This involves the use of a variable read_count, which is initially zero and counts the number of concurrent readers.

Channel 1 Message:

IF read_count > 0 THEN
   read_count := read_count − 1;
IF read_count = 0 THEN   {check for write requests}
   IF message on channel 2 THEN
      service write request on channel 2
   ELSE
      wait for message on any channel;

Channel 2 Message:

IF read_count > 0 THEN
   wait for message on channel 1 {'I've finished reading' messages}
ELSE
   send message ('OK to write')
   wait for message on channel 1; {'I've finished writing' message only}

Channel 3 Message:

read_count := read_count + 1;
send message ('OK to read');
wait for message on any channel; {Request or finished messages}

This simple algorithm exploits the fact that we can choose which channels we wish to wait for. When waiting for messages on a specific channel (say channel 1), it is quite probable that messages will be queued on the other channels waiting to be serviced. As the requesting processes are halted until they receive a reply to their messages, the message system provides an effective queuing mechanism for the halted processes.

12.5 Summary

Message passing provides another mechanism for achieving process synchronisation. Operating at a higher level than the semaphores described in chapter 10, message passing systems are equally suited for distributed processing across a network, tightly coupled systems or uni-processors. The chapter has examined the requirements of basic message passing operations and their use within a distributed system for remote procedure calls.

Various practical considerations in the implementation of a message passing system are discussed. These include the format of the message, the means of addressing destination processes, types of queuing discipline, message validation and deadlock avoidance. A solution to the reader's and writer's problem is presented to illustrate the use of a message passing capability.

12.6 References and bibliography

A.D. Birrell and B.J. Nelson (1984). 'Implementing Remote Procedure Calls', *ACM Transactions on Computer Systems*, Vol. 2, pp. 39-59.

J. Staustrup (1982). 'Message Passing Communication versus Procedure Call Communications', *Software - Practice and Experience*, Vol. 12, No. 3, pp. 223-34.

13 Networks and Interworking

13.1 Introduction to networks

The impact of networking computer systems together has been very significant. Helped by reductions in the cost of processors through technological developments, it is now cost effective to distribute the processing capability of a computer system to the locations which are most appropriate for it. This has impacted on the system configurations as a whole, the functionality of the system and how it is distributed across the network, and indeed, the 'added value' which the network itself may provide over and above that of the processing elements themselves. The wide acceptance of international standards has accelerated this process, allowing systems from many different manufacturers to be interconnected in a coherent way.

The change from a reliance on a centralised computer system to distributed computing reflects the changes that have come about within commercial organisations through increased use of information technology. Many companies have a substantial number of computers in operation, which may physically be widely separated. However, there is an increasing need to extract and correlate the information between these separate systems, thereby providing the potential for all programs, data and resources to be available to all users on the network without regard to their physical location.

This has additional benefits in terms of the overall system effectiveness, as having alternative sources of supply, it can be possible to continue operation even if one of the computers on the network has failed. Not only does this allow for graceful degradation in the event of part of the computer system failing, but it also provides a good path for upgrade and incremental expansion of the system.

An important consideration in the development of networks has been the impact of the relative pricing of computing to communications. Prior to 1970 computer hardware was so expensive that there were relatively few computers and data was brought to them for analysis. Since 1970 the cost has decreased and it is realistic to have computers to analyse the data at the location of the data source, and then send summary information to other sites.

There are many other by-products of networks, amongst which is the provision of a communication medium of widely separated people. Use of electronic mail and electronic conferencing are now widely used over communication networks.

A typical computer network interconnects many computers which are often referred to as hosts. Each host is capable of providing computing services to network users. The networks are connected by various types of communication links such as telephone lines, satellite links, coaxial cables, fibre optics and microwave links. They may also contain special communication processors, whose primary functions are:

(1) To effect the communication between the hosts
(2) To offload the communication tasks from the hosts
(3) To define the interface through which the host computers access the communication capabilities of the network.

Each host computer has an operating system which supports application processes. In addition there are operating systems which control computer networks which provide functions:

(1) To support terminal access to remote hosts
(2) To handle file transfer between hosts
(3) To handle inter-user communications such as electronic mail.

The main way of characterising networks is in terms of the distance that they cover, and this leads to two main classes of network - local area networks, or LANs, and wide area networks, or WANs. LANs cover an area which is not usually larger than a few kilometres, and are characterised by very high throughput and low end-to-end delay times. Typically they exist as networks within buildings, offices or other single sites. WANs cover a wide geographical area and are frequently used to network between sites, linking the LANs at each site together. Both private and public WANs exist, the latter being provided as a service in the same way as a telephone system.

The linking of computers together is complicated by two major factors. The first is that the computer systems themselves may be of a heterogeneous nature, from different manufacturers and running different system software. This is further complicated if the systems are connected to different networks, which are themselves inter-linked and which have different characteristics and protocols. For these reasons, the standardisation of network protocols and *gateways* between networks plays an important part in ensuring satisfactory interworking between the systems.

13.2   File transfers and mail systems

Computer networks are often used in one of two ways; firstly to move data files among a group of machines, and secondly to allow terminal users to log-on to remote machines. An extension of the former is the use of electronic mail between users. The main higher layer protocol for moving data between machines is that of a file transfer protocol.

The protocol to be discussed here is that based on the ARPANET (McQuillan and Walden, 1977) file transfer protocol. The protocol can be invoked in two different ways as illustrated in figure 13.1, depending on whether the person or process invoking the file transfer wishes to move a file between the local host to a remote machine, or to direct a transfer from one remote host to another. Commands which tell what to transfer, and where, may be sent over connections that differ from those used by the data.

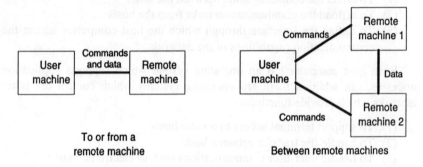

Figure 13.1   File transfer protocol model

Files are transferred for three main reasons:

(1) To store a file for subsequent retrieval
(2) To print a file, typically on a local printer
(3) To run the file as a program or process it as data.

Each of these categories has its own particular problems.

When a file is moved from one machine to another for storage, the only requirement is that when it is retrieved it must be reproduced exactly. This means that there must be no code conversion, even if the system is hetero-geneous and the machines themselves differ in parameters such as word length. If the word lengths are different then the file needs to be padded out with zero bits so as to fill an integral number of words. When the file is retrieved then its exact original size must be known.

When a file is transferred for printing there are more difficult problems to be solved. A character set conversion may be needed. Also some machines store print lines in different formats, such as variable length or fixed length, as well as using different carriage return and form feed encodings.

When a file is being transferred to be used as a program or data, the problems become even greater. If the file is a source program then usually a more specialised protocol is needed. Even if the file is a binary file there may still be serious problems with things such as word length, and form of arithmetic, such as one's or two's complement. A transformation is needed which preserves the semantics of the data.

Semantic invariance may be provided if each item is preceded by a header which tells what kind of information the item is, and perhaps how long the item is. This is illustrated in figure 13.2. Each block header identifies whether the item is an integer, floating point number, character string, bit string, or something else. With this information the file transfer protocol can attempt to change the representation to the one which is normally used by the receiving machine. This may be simple for integers, but conversion of floating point numbers is usually less straightforward.

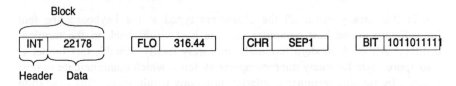

Figure 13.2   Data items for file transfer protocol

13.3   Networked terminals

There are many different types of terminals and, for computer network users, it is important that the programs they wish to use are able to communicate with their particular terminals. To satisfy this requirement, protocols have been devised whose function is to hide the differences between different kinds of terminals. Terminals fall into the categories:

(1) Simple character terminals
(2) Screen based terminals
(3) Virtual terminals
(4) Bit mapped terminals.

13.3.1 *Simple character terminals*

Simple character terminals, sometimes referred to as dumb terminals, can be connected to computer systems on point-to-point links. Characters may be transmitted over the connecting network asynchronously, using a simple arrangement such as that shown in figure 13.3.

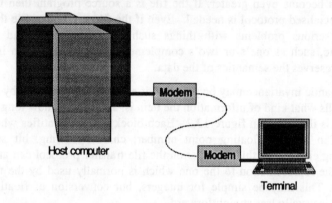

Figure 13.3   Simple dumb terminal attachment

In this arrangement, all the characters typed at the keyboard are sent immediately to the host computer and the host writes back to the terminal display. Although modern terminals are rarely totally 'dumb', this model is also appropriate for many microcomputer systems, which communicate to host systems by running terminal emulation programs within them, thus appearing as a simple terminal.

The slow nature of input/output with these terminals, for example at typing speed, means that a connection of this type would use only a small fraction of the available bandwidth of the modem link. This might be very costly to operate, for example if the telecommunications link was provided by the telephone system. To provide greater utilisation, a system such as that illustrated in figure 13.4 could be used. In this case, a **PAD** or packet assembler disassembler supports the more complex communication protocols to link a terminal on to an X.25 network.

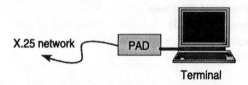

Figure 13.4   A terminal to PAD connection on to X.25.

13.3.2 Screen based terminals

This form of terminal differs from the simple character terminal in that it provides for a certain amount of local processing within the terminal to maintain the screen display, and interactions take place via the **total** screen, rather than on a character-by-character basis or a line-by-line basis.

In this form of operation, control effectively alternates between the host, which controls the screen, and the user, having control of the device. The concept is similar to interacting via a token, which is passed between the user and the host computer.

13.3.3 Virtual terminals

In the case of simple character and screen based terminals, the characteristics of the terminal and parameters associated with controlling it are known to the host system. An alternative approach is to view the terminal in an abstract way, removing from the host the need to know the physical characteristics of each terminal connected to it. A model has been developed which is intended to cope with the virtual terminal type. This is based on work by Schicker and Duenki (1978), and it is shown in outline in figure 13.5.

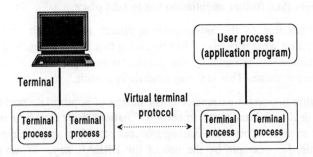

Figure 13.5 Conceptual model of the virtual terminal protocol

The terminal is driven by a terminal process which is either in the host computer or in the terminal itself. This process communicates with its opposite number on the remote machine. The application program, which is the user process, issues commands to the application process and gets replies from it. The terminal process and the application process exchange messages whose contents are determined by the virtual terminal protocol.

The basic idea of the virtual terminal protocol is that of the network virtual terminal or NVT. The NVT is a simple abstract terminal that responds to the printable ASCII characters and control characters such as line feed and carriage return. All other parameters and characteristics are regarded as strictly local to the terminal. Interactive application programs assume that their terminal is a network virtual terminal and drive it accordingly. In this model each terminal has a data structure. When an application process wants to send information to the terminal it issues commands to the application process. On receiving a command from the application program, the application process updates its copy of the data structure and then sends a message to the terminal process causing it to update its copy of the data structure in the same way. After having updated its data structure, the terminal process must then modify the display to make it correspond to the updated data structure. When the terminal user modifies the display, the terminal process must both update its own data structure and send update commands to the application process.

The virtual terminal protocol must ensure the consistency of the two data structures after every update. Whilst this concept of having identical data structures at both ends of a connection is good, it cannot hide all the differences associated with terminals. In order to establish who is willing to do what, and in order to change parameters from their default settings, the application and terminal processes need to perform an option negotiation. This may be achieved in different ways. In the asymmetric case, one side proposes to use certain options and the other side can either accept or reject them. If there is disagreement then further negotiation has to take place.

An alternative to the asymmetric approach is for each end to send a message stating what it needs. After receiving this message, each computes the lowest common denominator of the parameter settings and initialises its data structure to use these. This is the symmetric approach.

A further important parameter in the design of appropriate protocols is that of how to deal with interrupts. In certain situations there may be a need to stop the output stream. Most time-sharing systems provide a suitable mechanism to achieve this, for example by the use of the BREAK key. When there is no network involved then the operating system can readily dispose of all queued output and remember not to display anything until the current process has terminated.

There is a problem when a BREAK has to be sent over the network. If the terminal simply relays the BREAK to the other side without discarding queued output, then printing may continue for a long time owing to output which has been previously generated and now is queued up in the terminal process. This can lead to a long recovery time which will exist even if the BREAK message is sent out of band and allowed to skip past other messages that are queued up for the application process.

If alternatively the terminal process discards all queued and incoming characters as well as the incoming BREAK, it has no way of knowing when to start displaying characters again. In particular, it cannot distinguish between the remote command interpreter's prompt character and the same sequence sent by the rogue process itself. Also the process may catch BREAK signals and process them itself, in which case there is no prompt at all.

One solution to this problem with handling interrupts is to have the recipient of an interrupt message insert a special mark into the output stream. However if both sides simultaneously transmit interrupts then a more complex protocol is needed to decide whose turn it is. In any event, when a process has sent an interrupt message it updates the state variable in the data structure in order to remember that it has done so, returning to the normal state only after the interrupt protocol has finished.

In a typical implementation, the application program would be provided with library routines or system calls as well as some mechanism for interrogating the current state of the virtual terminal. In this way the program could manipulate the cursor and use the different renditions without even being aware of the terminal-dependent codes needed to invoke these facilities.

13.3.4 Bit mapped terminals

Bit mapped terminals are those where each point, or pixel, on the screen is mapped on to one or more bits of computer memory. Complete control of the display is possible and, within the limits of screen resolution, any arbitrary picture may be displayed by setting suitable pixel values. Such terminals are particularly suitable for window management systems, using principles such as those presented by Hopgood (1986).

The development of window systems has allowed user interfaces based on WIMPs, or Windows, Icons, Menus and Pointers. Details of such systems are discussed in Goldberg (1988). Most early systems relied upon the interface being implemented in the same machine as the application, so that the user process could interact directly with the window in memory.

More recent developments are more amenable to network operation, and windowing systems based on X-windows and NEWS provide a similar capability in a network environment.

13.4 ISO models

Many networks are designed in a highly structured manner, and several of these are organised as a series of layers or levels each of which is built upon its predecessor. The number of layers and their individual functions vary from network to network. However, in all networks, the purpose of each layer is to provide certain services for the higher layers thereby shielding, or hiding, the details as to how these services are actually implemented. Thus layer n on one machine carries on conversation with layer n on another machine, and the rules and convention of this conversation are defined in the layers n protocol. The entities which comprise the corresponding layers on different machines are called peer processes. This peer process abstraction is crucial in network design. It is through this that the design can be partitioned into smaller, manageable units which form the design of the individual layers. The set of layers and protocols is called the network architecture.

In practice, no data can be transferred directly from layer n on one machine to layer n on another, except at the lowest of the levels. Each layer passes data and control information to the layer immediately below it until the lowest level is reached. It is at this lowest level that physical communication with another machine can take place rather than the virtual communication that is used by the higher levels.

Between each pair of adjacent layers there is an interface. This interface defines which primitive operations and services the lower layer offers to the higher one at the interface. It is important that when protocols are defined, there are clearly defined interfaces for each of the layers.

There are many issues in the design of the layers. Each layer must have the mechanism for the establishment of communications, together with the ability to address many destinations. Not only is there a need to establish the means of communication, there is also the need to be able to terminate the communications. In addition, the means of data transfer needs to be specified, whether it is uni-directional as in simplex, or half duplex as two way alternate communication, or to allow simultaneous communication in two directions as full duplex.

Error detection and correction are also important and various techniques exist to address these problems. There is also need to control the ordering of messages, that is to provide a measure of sequencing. It is also necessary to control the situation if one sender sends data much faster than a slower receiver which it may swamp, or lead to starvation.

There is a need to provide a mechanism to handle variable-length messages, as in practice they may be arbitrarily long. However, an alternative problem can arise if the data units are so small that sending them at that size becomes very inefficient because of the overheads for each data transfer.

It may be inefficient or expensive to provide communications between each pair of processes, so that the same connection may be used for multiple, unrelated conversations. Such a system provides multiplexing of the data transfers.

There are many protocols, but the model which is to be considered is that developed by the International Standards Organisation (ISO). The Reference Model of Open Systems Interconnection (OSI) has seven layers. Zimmermann (1980) discusses the principles which have been used to arrive at the seven layers, and some of the major points are:

(1) A layer should be created where a different level of abstraction is needed.
(2) Each layer should perform a well defined function which should be chosen with a view toward defining internationally standardised protocols.
(3) The layer boundaries should be chosen to minimise the information flow across the interfaces.
(4) The number of layers should be large enough that distinct functions need not be brought together in the same layer out of necessity, and also be small enough that the architecture does not become too unwieldy.

Figure 13.6 shows the layers of the ISO Model. Each of the layers has a well defined function, and these are described briefly.

1 Physical layer

This is the level at which the interchange of electrical signals which represent data and control information takes place. This layer includes the specification of the electrical and mechanical characteristics of the physical connection. Also defined are the procedures for the establishing, maintaining and releasing of connections between electrical circuits which are linked by the communications medium. Examples of standards at this level include the popular RS-232C and IEEE 488 protocols, albeit under their ISO nomenclature of V.24.

2 Data link layer

This layer takes the bare bit-level communication system which is provided by the physical layer and superimposes on it a means of transmitting data and control information. The protocol used may be character-oriented in which case control characters are used to delimit the various fields of the basic transmission block, or it may rely on positional significance. The acknow-

ledgment of data receipt and error control are both implemented at this level
which also provides the facility to retransmit the data and control information if
necessary. Flow control to prevent fast devices swamping slower devices may
also be provided a this level. Examples of the standards at this level are the
HDLC (high-level data link control) which is used on X.25 point-to-point links,
ADCCP (advanced data communication control procedures), SDLC
(synchronous data link control) and IEEE 802.3 link level control.

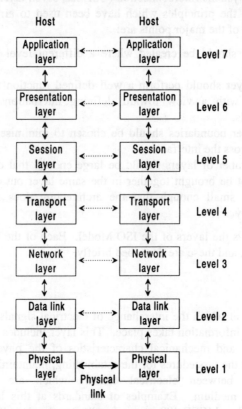

Figure 13.6   Host to host communication using the ISO 7 layer model

3 Network layer

This layer of the hierarchy takes the packet-sized data blocks that are handed
down from the transport layer and attaches to these the address and routing
information which completes the packet. The choice of routing algorithm is
arbitrary so that routing can be fixed or adaptive which allows packets to be
routed according to current network traffic loads. Routing can be limited to a

single network or be extended to transfer packets between interconnected networks.

4 Transport layer

Layer 4 and above in the OSI model are concerned with end-to-end communication, and so are largely independent of the underlying telecommunication facilities. Layer 4 provides a reliable data transmission and reception service for the session layer. The data is transmitted in the most efficient way that is suitable for the needs of the session layer. This may be an error-free virtual connection with acknowledgments on a per-packet basis for secure data exchange. It could also be a transmission service with no guarantee of delivery, which may be suitable for certain types of traffic such as digital voice. The transport layer takes data from the session layer and splits it into pieces which are the size of the packet data field. It then passes these data blocks to the network layer. An example of this layer is TCP (Transmission Control Protocol).

5 Session layer

This layer provides a service to establish, maintain and terminate a connection with a process in a remote host computer. The layer should provide a reliable service to the presentation layer and have the ability to re-establish a connection should one of the lower layers in the hierarchy fail. During the establishment of a connection, the session layer must be able to negotiate with the remote machine over certain connection parameters. These parameters may include the types of communications that are to be used, such as full duplex or half duplex, how the integrity of the session connection is controlled and the quality of service which is to be expected by the session users.

6 Presentation layer

This layer provides a set of services to the application layer which can be used to process the data exchanged across the session connection. The presentation layer defines the syntax used between the application entities and provides for the selection and subsequent modification of the representation to be used. Examples of presentation protocols are teletex, videotex, virtual terminal protocol and encryption.

7 Application layer

This is the highest layer in the network architecture. The layer interacts directly with the application software which is wanting to transfer data across the network. All the other layers in the hierarchy exist for the sole purpose of satisfying the needs of this layer, and the physical characteristics of the underlying network are hidden by these other layers. Examples of protocols at this layer are file transfer and manipulation protocol, job transfer and manipulation protocol, and X.400 mail protocol.

This OSI standard is only a model. Very few local networks adhere strictly to this 7-level hierarchy. In some cases, layers may be missing because they may not be needed in that particular system, and in others the functions normally associated with a particular layer may be performed by a different layer.

13.5 Summary

Networks and interworking provide greater effectiveness for computer systems by allowing information transfer and the option of remotely distributed processing. In this context, the operating system requirements of the associated network are largely concerned with the importance of compatibility and the needs for standards to maintain functionality. Networks can be classified into two main types, namely local area networks (LANs) and wide area networks (WANs).

In this chapter, several principles of interworking have been outlined, in particular those associated with file transfer and mail systems, as well as the different types of access which are provided by a range of terminals. Finally the different layers of the ISO 7 layer model of network protocols have been considered briefly, so as to highlight the functionality provided by each of the layers.

13.6 References and bibliography

V.G. Cerf and E. Cain (1983). 'The DOD Internet Architecture Model', *Computer Networks*, Vol. 7, No. 5, pp. 307-318.

M. Gien (1978). 'A File Transfer Protocol FTP', *Computer Networks*, Vol. 2, No. 4/5, pp. 312-9.

A. Goldberg (1988), *A History of Personal Workstations*, ACM Press.

F.R.A. Hopgood *et al* (eds) (1988), *Methodology of Window Management*, Springer Verlag.

J.M. McQuillan and D.C. Walden (1977), 'The ARPA Network Design Decisions', *Computer Networks*, Vol. 1, pp. 243-289.

J.S. Quarterman (1990). *The Matrix Computer Networks and Conferencing Systems Worldwide*, Digital Press, Medford, Mass.

P. Schicker and A. Duenki (1978), 'The Virtual Terminal Definition', *Computer Networks*, Vol. 2, pp. 429-441.

H. Zimmermann (1980), 'OSI Reference Model - The ISO Model of Architecture for Open Systems Interconnections', *IEEE Trans. Comms.*, COM-28(4), pp. 425-432.

14 Operating System Performance

14.1 Functions and constraints of a system

Throughout this book, there has been emphasis placed on the management of resources within an operating system, and on how effectively this management is performed. Through technological developments, the good utilisation of resources has become a less critical issue than in the early days of computing when processing power and memory were extremely expensive commodities. Nevertheless, the behaviour of computer systems as a whole is still of great concern. In many applications, the demand for processing capability is insatiable, and the wise and efficient usage of resources is still therefore a major issue for system designers.

In this chapter, we examine how we can assess whether a computer system is achieving its goals in terms of its overall performance. The assessments tend to be relative rather than absolute measures. They are frequently used for evaluation purposes prior to selection of a computer system, or to monitor the extent to which a system achieves its design goals, particularly after development or change. Whilst many of the measures of performance, such as the number of transactions processed per unit time or the number of terminals that can be supported, may be regarded as absolute measures of performance, in practice, such information is normally used as a comparative indicator.

Before considering the parameters that may be used as measures of performance, it is worth noting some of the purposes to which such indications may be used. Some of the common purposes are:

(1) Selection evaluation - to aid decisions about systems before purchase

(2) Performance projection - to aid forward planning about the future requirements for a computer system and the suitability of projected configurations

(3) Performance monitoring - to check that a system is meeting its goals, and to provide data for future strategic decision taking.

196

Performance evaluation and prediction are needed from the time of conception of future systems, through monitoring their running, to planning for future enhancements and upgrades, and then to the final subsequent replacement.

In the early stages of a system design, there is a need to consider the nature of the applications that are to be run on the system, together with the likely workloads that will arise. Subsequently, performance evaluation and prediction will be used to provide the optimal hardware configuration, the resource management strategies that the operating system will need to use, and whether or not the system achieves its performance objectives.

In order to attain the best performance, each computer system may have to be adjusted to optimise its use in that particular situation. Such changes are often referred to as customisation of the system and can be undertaken in the configuration process. Any subsequent fine-tuning may be made within the user's operating environment and this stage is usually called system tuning.

14.2 Performance of a simple system

Whilst some of the performance parameters are easily quantifiable, such as the number of jobs per unit time, others, such as ease of use, are not so easily quantified. Still others, such as response time, may be strongly user-oriented rather than system-oriented, and are expressed in terms of what is regarded as acceptable for the particular system.

In consideration of the performance and utilisation of a system, many parameters may be included. Frequently encountered parameters are:

(1) CPU utilisation
(2) Throughput
(3) Turnaround time
(4) Waiting time
(5) Response time

In a multiprogramming system, it is the concern of the operating system to decide which process to run at any time. This decision is based on parameters such as those above, and is the subject of scheduling algorithms which were described in detail in chapter 4. However at this stage it is useful to explain the significance of these simple functions in relation to overall performance.

CPU utilisation is the average fraction of the time during which the CPU is busy. In this context, being busy may include both the time spent executing the user programs and the time executing the operating system on behalf of the user, but not idle time. The obvious aim is to keep the CPU busy for 100 per cent of the time.

Throughput refers to the amount of work completed per unit time. One way to express this is the number of user jobs completed per unit time. In this case the higher the number, the greater the apparent work which is being done by the system. However, such a measurement may be misleading since it is strongly dependent on the nature of the jobs that are being processed, for example, whether they are long batch jobs or short highly interactive jobs, as may occur while programs are being developed. To provide an effective comparison between systems using this as a measure would need the same job profiles to be executed.

Turnaround time may be expressed as the time which elapses from the moment that a job, or program, is submitted until it is completed by the system. This is only a realistic parameter in the case of batch operation.

Waiting time is the time that a job spends waiting for resource allocation due to contention with other jobs. It may be expressed as the turnaround time minus the actual execution time of the job. Whilst this seems to give a similar measure as turnaround time, waiting time attempts to remove variability which is included due to the job's execution time. For example, a long job running with no preemptions may have the same turnaround time as a short job with many preemptions, whereas the waiting times will be very different, and in this case would give a better interpretation of performance.

Response time is usually of importance in the case of time-sharing and real-time systems. In the time-sharing case the response time can simply represent the time taken between the last character entered on a screen and the first results appearing on the screen, and is sometimes called the terminal response time. For real-time systems, the response time is the time between when an event is signalled until the first instruction of its respective service routine is executed, and is sometimes called the event response time.

Whilst these and other parameters may be used as a measure of performance, it is also worth noting that many of the values may have a wide range of variance. In some of the cases, knowledge of such variance can give additional information about the performance of the system. For example, in the case of response time, the variance gives a measure of the dispersion so that a small variance shows that all the users experience the same response time around the mean value, whereas a large variance shows that some users will experience a fast response whilst others suffer from a very slow response. From the users' point of view, information of such variance is a significant measure for an interactive system.

The probabilistic nature of some of the parameters such as response time means that they are considered as random variables in the performance evaluation which may, for example, be based on simulation. Suitable probability distributions can accurately reflect the variance that exists.

14.3 Performance evaluation

Just as there are numerous parameters that may be used to measure performance, so there are various techniques which may be used for performance evaluation. The most common ones used at present are:

(1) Raw timings

These provide a quick comparison of computer hardware and are often characterised in such units as MIPs (millions of instructions per second) for processing power, or as MFLOPs (millions of floating point operations per second) where floating point operations are appropriate. Since these refer to machine instructions, it is often hard to use this as a meaningful comparison between systems where different implementations of machine instructions exist (as in RISC v CISC architectures).

(2) Instruction mixes

These provide a weighted average of various instruction timings. With greater use of pipelining and cache memory in hardware, such comparisons are getting less meaningful since the same operation may take a range of timings dependent on the context of the operation.

(3) Kernel programs

Execution times calculated for specific systems are used as a basis for comparison. This attempts to remove the difficulties of timing and instruction mixes.

(4) Analytic models

Models are used to simulate the operation of the computer system. These may use models, such as queuing theory and Markov processes. The models can become extremely complex and difficult to represent in all but the simplest systems.

(5) Benchmarks

In this case performance is assessed against the timing for the execution of a real program, unlike the case of kernel programs, which were based on calculated execution timings. Some care is needed in assessment of results from benchmark measurements since the results may be strongly influenced by whether the system is optimised for that style of job; for example, vector processing machines will show considerable benefits if using matrix multiplication as the benchmark program. Specially developed programs for systems are often referred to as synthetic programs.

(6) Simulation

This is where a computerised model of the system being evaluated is developed. By this technique it is possible to develop a model of a system based on certain circumstances and then run the model to see how the system will perform under these circumstances. Using simulation may highlight problems that can arise and which could lead to poor utilisation of a system. Simulators are usually based on two types:

(a) Event-driven which are controlled by events that are produced using probability distributions

(b) Data-driven which are controlled by empirically derived data that is constructed to reflect the anticipated behaviour of the system.

Simulation techniques usually produce large amounts of data and require large amounts of computing time.

14.4 Performance monitoring

Performance monitoring refers to the collection and analysis of information which relates to the performance of existing systems. It provides information about how the system is performing in relation to such parameters as response time, throughput and CPU usage. Such monitoring should provide operators with information about bottle-necks and provide the information on which management can base decisions about how to improve performance.

The style of jobs can strongly influence the performance and the potential for improvement. In the case of production jobs, time spent developing optimising compilers may be beneficial; however, for the case of short jobs, program development and debugging, then simple compilers may suffice.

Performance monitoring may be accomplished either by hardware or software. Usually such monitoring techniques generate large amounts of data for subsequent analysis. Some care needs to be taken when deciding the level and extent of monitoring that is to be undertaken.

In some situations there are advantages to undertaking a trace of the program execution. This can be particularly useful to highlight the occurrence of bottle-necks, and areas of the execution which may benefit from optimisation to improve system performance.

14.5 Usability of a simple system

Within a computer system, the operating system manages the collection of resources. One of the potential problems that can arise is that one or more of the resources may become a bottle-neck. This will limit the overall performance of the system since the bottle-neck can mean that while some resources are being underused, the effect of the bottle-neck can be to prevent the progress of processes or jobs requiring these underused resources.

Usually a bottle-neck situation starts to arise as the utilisation of that particular resource reaches saturation. In the case of paging, this effect leads to thrashing, which was described in chapter 6. In thrashing, the working sets for a given set of processes cannot be maintained simultaneously in main storage.

In order to detect bottle-necks, monitoring the queues for each resource can be used to detect the build-up towards saturation. Such a build-up occurs when the service rate for that particular resource is much less than the arrival rate for input to that resource. Having detected the presence of a bottle-neck, the bottle-neck may be removed by the provision of additional resources. However there is then the possibility that fresh bottle-necks will appear elsewhere in the system.

The performance in the operating system is often sensitive to the current state of the system. By continual monitoring of the system, there is the possibility of using feedback of this information to improve performance. This use of information, such as the arrival rates, is sometimes referred to as feedback. Feedback can be used in either a positive or a negative sense. In positive feedback the information can lead to an increase of the arrival rate to give better use of a particular resource. In the case of negative feedback the arrival rate may be decreased to reduce the likelihood of a bottle-neck developing for a particular resource.

Whilst negative feedback can lead to stability in queues for resources, use of positive feedback needs more care. One of the potentially serious problems that can arise from positive feedback is the possibility of instabilities developing. Such problems mean that great care is needed in the allocation of resources to avoid the consequence of bottle-necks arising.

14.6   Summary

With any engineered product, it is important to be able to assess the performance and quality of the system, to know its limitations and future potential. This applies to software systems as much as the products from any other engineering discipline. In the case of operating systems, the importance of being able to assess the system is even more significant, as poor operating system performance is often highlighted through the running of end-user applications.

This chapter has considered various aspects of performance evaluation of operating systems. It has identified system parameters which are of interest to both designers and system managers, such as utilisation, throughput, turnaround time, waiting time and response time. It has also discussed various techniques for evaluating the performance, from measurement of raw instruction times through to modelling and simulation. The use of the operating system itself to collect performance statistics and to use this information within adaptive strategies is also identified.

14.7   References and bibliography

R.P. Weicker (1990). 'An Overview of Common Benchmarks', *Computer*, Vol. 23, No. 12, pp.65-76.

Appendix - An example system

The aim throughout this book has been to introduce the basic concepts which underpin the design of any operating system. It is recognised by the authors that few readers will ever be involved in developing major operating systems themselves. For this reason, actual systems, such as UNIX, have only been examined in a cursory way to illustrate the basic principles of operating system design. A detailed study of any one operating system could more than fill a text book and an associated lecture course, so the temptation to focus on one particular system has been avoided.

Equally, it is recognised that many software developers will undertake the production of more specialised system software, particularly for wide classes of embedded systems and control applications. In many respects, these exhibit the characteristics of simple operating systems, unfettered by the constraints imposed by the requirements of generality. Although such systems are often produced in an *ad hoc* way to meet the very specific needs identified at the outset, to all intents and purposes they are operating systems in their own right.

This appendix is intended to reinforce the material covered earlier in this book, by providing a pseudo-code outline of various components of a simple operating system. A Pascal-like notation has been used where appropriate. The design is based on the structure of the simple time-sharing system introduced in chapter 2, and is elaborated further through the functionality introduced in subsequent chapters, for example, those concerned with process scheduling and memory management.

The design introduced is intended to be relatively complete as an illustration of a possible system, although it is recognised that, with the range of techniques and algorithms available to system software developers, its use for more than illustrative purposes is limited. Exercises involving further development of the basic system are also identified.

The following figure, based on the system in chapter 2, illustrates the components to be examined. The system would be capable of servicing a small cluster of terminals, with a spooling facility for output documents to a printer. Networking facilities, such as remote job submission, have been omitted.

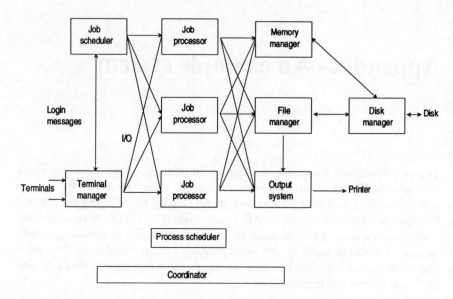

The software can be broadly grouped into the categories:

1 Scheduling   **3 I/O Systems**
   1.1 Job Scheduler   3.1 Terminal Manager
   1.2 Process Scheduler   3.2 Output System
   1.3 Coordinator

2 Storage management   **4 Job Processor**
   2.1 Memory Manager
   2.2 Disk Manager
   2.3 File Manager

A modular approach has been chosen in specifying the software of the system, so that the procedures and data structures associated with a particular function are encapsulated within a program module.

Procedures within a module may take two forms. The first is as the main body of a process, which runs as an autonomous thread of execution. The second is as interface procedures, which allow processes to interact and request services of other processes. The interface procedures will normally run in the context (execution environment) of the calling process, often manipulating shared data structures, and would only free the called process if an independent activity was required.

A1 Scheduling

Three levels of scheduling were identified and discussed in chapter 4. At the highest level is the Job Scheduler, which is concerned with the allocation of Job Processors. It therefore responds to users as they log-in on terminals and validates user entry into the system. The middle level of scheduling is provided by the Process Scheduler, which is responsible for the allocation of time slices to each Job Processor, as required. Finally, the lowest level of scheduling is provided by the Coordinator. This is concerned with the rapid switching between all the processes in the system and for implementing appropriate halting and freeing mechanisms to enable processes to interact.

A1.1 Job Scheduler

In a large system, the Job Scheduler would be concerned with assigning processes (Job Processors) to tasks arriving from a number of sources, namely:

 i)   users at terminals, requiring interactive facilities,
 ii) jobs submitted from remote terminals and machines across a network,
 iii) work initiated locally by the users/processes wishing to have background tasks running on their behalf.

Given that the resources of a system are bounded, the maximum number of processes which might be supported is likely to be defined by a system configuration parameter. Potentially this number could be considerably less than the maximum required for tasks originating from all sources. Under these circumstances, work for the system would have to be queued and users might be prevented from logging in while the system was overloaded. Naturally, the scheduler would tend to give preference to the interactive workload originating from local terminals.

In this simple example, it has been assumed that the only source of work comes via the terminals. As these are also physical resources of the system, whose number is bounded, reasonable limits can be applied to the number of processes allowed in the system such that the problem of overloading is avoided. In principle, a direct one-to-one association could exist between terminals and Job Processors, thereby eliminating the role of the Job Scheduler almost entirely. The only function remaining would be the login procedure, which could equally well be performed within the Job Processors themselves. However, the Job Scheduler has been retained in this example on the assumption that background tasks might ultimately be supported.

job scheduler:
```
REPEAT
    WHILE no terminal input DO wait
        {Job scheduler communicates with the terminal manager      }
        {when a terminal is not logged in                          }
    select data structures for the terminal with input
    IF waiting for username THEN
        read username
        prompt for password
    IF waiting for password THEN
        read password
    IF username and password valid THEN
        allocate job processor
        notify terminal manager of the job processor identity and
        notify job processor of the terminal identity
        {All further input / output is between the job processor    }
        {and the terminal manager, until the user logs out          }
        wake (job processor)
        {Inform process scheduler that the job processor            }
        {can be allocated a time slice                              }
    ELSE
        monitor invalid login
        wait for username to be typed
FOREVER
```

An interface procedure is required to notify the various system processes that a process has terminated and the user has logged out. This would allow the Job Processor to be reallocated.

terminate:
```
    {Called by a job processor when a user logs out}
    note that the current job processor is free
    notify the terminal manager that the user has logged out
    {Subsequent input / output will be with the job scheduler       }
    suspend (job processor)
    {Inform the process scheduler to disregard the current          }
    {job processor from any time slice scheduling                   }
    free (job scheduler)
    {Only if a queue of work waiting for a job processor is possible }
```

A1.2 Process Scheduler

The Process Scheduler is concerned with the allocation of time slices to the user processes running inside Job Processors. The scheme proposed here is a very simple Round Robin algorithm, which examines a data structure, *process list*, to identify the Job Processors which are free and may be allocated a time slice.

process scheduler:
```
    REPEAT
        process no := 0
        REPEAT
            IF free processes > 0 THEN
                IF process list [process no] = free THEN
                    current job processor := process no
                    set timer to time slice period
                    {This might be an actual hardware register, or a    }
                    {register value saved with the process context       }
                    free (job processor)
                    wait
                    {Halt the job scheduler until a time slice has completed }
                    {or until the job processor suspends itself,            }
                    {such as when waiting for input/output                  }
                    process no := process no + 1
            ELSE
                wait
                {No job processors to schedule                          }
            UNTIL process no > max job processors
            {Repeat cyclic scan of process list                      }
    FOREVER
```

Interface procedures are necessary within this module to control the suspension and waking of a Job Processor. There is also a procedure to service timer interrupts in order to end a time slice.

wake (process no):
```
    process list [process no] := free
    free processes := free processes + 1
    IF free processes = 1 THEN
        free (process scheduler)
        {Process scheduler would  have been waiting               }
        {with no job processors to schedule                       }
```

suspend:
> *{Called by a job processor to suspend itself}*
>
> process list [current job processor] := halted
> free (process scheduler)

timer:
> free (process scheduler)
> *{The coordinator will switch from the current job processor,   }*
> *{allowing the process scheduler to select a different   }*
> *{job processor to time slice   }*

A1.3 Coordinator

The Coordinator is responsible for scheduling the system processes and providing suitable synchronisation mechanisms to allow them to interact. The scheduling itself may be very simple, as rapid process changing within the operating system is essential. Typically two operations will be provided for use by the other processes; a Wait operation which halts the current process and enters the coordinator scheduler, and a Free operation to wake up another process if a service or interaction is required.

In order to keep the scheduling simple, the main data structure will be a *task list*, ordered on priority, with one entry for each operating system process and one entry for the current Job Processor. The nomenclature used in the pseudo-code is to refer to this subset of the total processes in the system as tasks.

coordinator:
```
REPEAT
    task no := 0
    {Tasks ordered on priority, so initialise circular scan        }
    REPEAT
        IF task list [task no] = free THEN
            current task := task no
            restore registers and re-enter process
            {Task executes and returns by calling wait             }
        task no := task no + 1
    UNTIL task no > max task number
    {This is the idle loop of the system, with the coordinator     }
    {repeatedly cycling, looking for tasks to run                  }
FOREVER
```

wait:

    save registers
    task list [current task] := halted
    reenter the coordinator

free (task):

    task list [task] := free
    IF current task = job processor THEN
        {Preemptive scheduling for the user processes   }
        save registers
        reenter the coordinator

A2 Storage management

Management of storage in this system is handled by three separate processes. The Memory Manager is concerned with maintaining the virtual store of the processes and the allocation of space in the RAM. The Disk Manager allocates space on the disk and performs transfers on behalf of other processes to and from the disk. Finally the File Manager is responsible for directory management, recording the addresses of the disk blocks which make up a file, and providing a suitable set of user commands for file manipulation (create, delete etc.).

There is naturally substantial interaction between these processes. Both the Memory Manager and File Manager make extensive use of the disk for paging and file storage. On some systems, the File Manager might map open files directly into the virtual store, so that they may be accessed in the same way as any scratch segment. Within this example system, an attempt has been made to keep the interactions down to a minimum and thus maintain simplicity.

A2.1 Memory Manager

The Memory Manager has two distinct functions. The first is to implement a virtual store for each process, maintaining a suitable set of address translation tables, such as those described in chapter 6 for a paged segmented system. Facilities to allow a user process to manipulate its virtual store, for example by creating segments and changing access permissions to them, would be implemented as a set of interface procedures for manipulating the segment tables and page tables. Its second role is the management of space in the RAM.

The software for the Memory Manager falls into three categories. The first is an independent process for implementing the store rejection algorithm. This creates free space for subsequent use by all the processes in the system and is the hub of the RAM management system, along with an interface procedure for allocating pages. The user functions, implemented via system calls to the interface procedures, are a very open ended set of facilities. In the interests of simplicity, this system assumes a rather static virtual store with few facilities for manipulating it. The final category is the software for implementing demand paging. This appears as an interrupt procedure for servicing virtual store interrupts when the address translation hardware is unable to locate a particular page in memory. This is treated as an exception condition within the current process rather than being an independent activity, and therefore appears as an interface procedure which is invoked autonomously by the hardware.

store rejection:
    {The main process of the memory manager}

    REPEAT
        page no := 0
        REPEAT
            WHILE free space available < threshold
                {Maintain a small pool of free space (threshold)}
                {Count pages being rejected as part of the free space}
                IF page [page no] is in use   *{do not reject free pages}*
                        AND page [page no] is NOT locked in THEN
                        {Such as page tables or pages involved in}
                        {autonomous peripheral transfers}
                        IF page [page no] has been referenced THEN
                            reset use information (referenced bit)
                        ELSE
                            {Page has not been referenced since}
                            {it was last considered for rejection}
                            make entry on disk transfer queue
                            {To remove the page}
                            mark this page as 'in transit'
                            {If a copy of the page is already on disk and it has}
                            {not been altered, the page may be freed immediately}
            page no := page no + 1
        UNTIL page no > RAM size
        {Repeat cyclic scan of pages of RAM}
    FOREVER

virtual store interrupt:

    IF segment undefined
        {Found by examining the process segment table   *}*
        OR required address > segment limit THEN
        fault current process
    ELSE   *{required address is valid, so retrieve the page*   *}*
        IF page table not in memory THEN
            reset 'required address' to retrieve page table
            {Page tables are paged in the same way as pages   *}*
        IF required page on disk THEN
            find an empty page of RAM
            make entry on disk transfer queue   *{To fetch the page*   *}*
            set page table status as 'in transit'
            note current process waiting for this page
            wait
        ELSE IF required page 'in transit' THEN
            add current process to queue waiting for this page
            wait
        ELSE
            {Page undefined, so allocate one   *}*
            find an empty page of RAM
            clear the page
            {The previous contents are unknown, so it is   *}*
            {more secure to set them to a predefined value   *}*
            set page table entry to point to the page
            RETURN
            {Returning from the interrupt allows the   *}*
            {current process to retry the failing instruction   *}*

find an empty page:

    IF no free space available THEN
        free (virtual store manager)
        {To create free space through the store rejection algorithm   *}*
        note current process waiting for space
        wait
        {The current process will be freed when a page has been rejected }
    allocate a page of RAM
    IF free space available < rejection threshold THEN
        free (virtual store manager)
        {This is an optimisation, to create free space before we run out   *}*
    RETURN

A2.2 Disk Manager

The Disk Manager coordinates access to the disk, reading and writing
input/output blocks on behalf of the File Manager and Virtual Store Manager.
It is also responsible for managing the free space on the disk, allocating blocks
when requested and recovering free space when blocks are no longer required.
The software would include an interrupt procedure for driving the disk, and
interface procedures to request transfers and manage the allocation and
recovery of space.

disk interrupt:

> IF transfer failed THEN
> > retry transfer
> > *{A more sophisticated error recovery could be implemented*   *}*
> IF store rejection transfer *{write}* THEN
> > note RAM page is now free
> > free processes waiting for space
> > update page table status to show page on disk
> > free any process waiting for this page of virtual store
> > *{This might be optimised, so that if a process*   *}*
> > *{tries to access a page which is being rejected,*   *}*
> > *{the page is not released when the transfer is completed*   *}*
> IF demand loading of page *{read}* THEN
> > update page table status to show page in RAM
> > free all processes waiting for this page of virtual store
> IF disk transfer queue is NOT empty THEN
> > remove entry from queue
> > start transfer

request disk transfer:

> insert transfer details into the disk transfer queue
> *{Details include RAM address, disk address, size and direction*   *}*
> IF disk is NOT busy THEN
> > start transfer
> > *{If the disk is already in transfer, the interrupt procedure*   *}*
> > *{will eventually service the request*   *}*

The interface procedures to request and release a disk block might operate
using a simple Boolean vector *block list*, with an entry corresponding to each
block on the disk. A Next Fit algorithm is an efficient implementation for the
request, so a cyclic pointer, *next block*, identifies the next candidate for
consideration.

request disk block:

```
WHILE block list [next block] <> free DO
    {cyclic scan of block list                              }
    next block := next block + 1
    IF next block = disk size THEN
        next block := 0
    block list [next block] := allocated
    RETURN (next block)
```

release disk block (block no):

```
block list [block no] := free
```

A2.3 File Manager

Although the File Manager and the Disk Manager are quite closely related, logically they have very different responsibilities. The Disk Manager is primarily concerned with the allocation of space on the disk and arranging for data transfers, whereas the File Manager is concerned with mapping the space in a useful way through its file directories. The security of files and associated accounting functions also fall within the remit of the File Manager.

A similar relationship might exist between the File Manager and software concerned with interpreting the contents of a file. For example, a Record Manager might support access to files in a structured way, such as Pascal records. This system adopts the approach used in a number of operating systems, including UNIX, in that it views the files as a simple sequence of characters with any further structuring imposed by application software.

The functionality of the File Manager is primarily concerned with providing an appropriate interface for users to manipulate files, either from the job command language or from within their own processes. It is therefore comprised almost entirely of interface procedures. The only functions which would merit a separate File Manager process running asynchronously would be activities such as file system validation at the time of starting the system or archiving facilities. Details of such processes have not been included in this design.

The overall functionality of this system has been assumed to be similar to that of many other systems. The interface procedures which allow manipulation of the file system are as follows:

Directory Manipulation:
      Create directory
      Delete directory
      Change directory   - identify a new origin for file path names

File Manipulation:
      Create file
      Open file   - for an existing file
      Close file   - possibly updating it
      Delete file
      Rename file

Internal File Structuring and Access:
      Read file block   - for accessing a page at a time
      Write file block
      In char   - for accessing a character at a time
      Out char

The range of facilities is clearly very open-ended. Many functions found in typical systems, such as the copying of files or record management operations, could be provided very easily using the basic primitive functions identified. Pseudo code has not been provided for the File Manager interface procedures as the overall functionality is simple and relatively obvious.

A3 I/O Systems

Although the system is primarily supporting terminals, facilities may still be provided for printing documents on a printer or inputting a file or job via a communications link. The Output System would naturally be included within the design to provide a printing capability. However, as networking is not supported within this simple example, the Input System has been omitted entirely.

A3.1 Terminal Manager

The Terminal Manager buffers single characters or single lines of input data in RAM. The first line typed by a user is sent from the Terminal Manager to the Job Scheduler. This normally identifies the user and provides any security checks (password checking) and charging information that may be required as part of the normal sequence for logging-in to the system. All subsequent input and output operations are then made directly between the Terminal Manager and the Job Processor.

The design assumes a functionality similar to that described in chapter 3. Each terminal has an identical set of data structures assigned to it. The terminal input uses a cyclic buffering scheme, with variables *bufinptr, bufinlin, userinptr* and *userinlin* to identify the current lines being typed and processed. This implementation would only wake the user process when a complete line of input were available (not on each character). The buffering process is interrupt driven and an interface procedure, read ch, may be called to remove characters from the buffer.

For terminal output, a more simple system would suffice so only two pointers, *bufoutptr* and *useroutptr*, are needed to access a cyclic buffer. Once again the buffering process is interrupt driven with an interface procedure, write ch, being called by the user process to output characters.

Two generic functions have been assumed in order to assist in the management of the cyclic buffer pointers. These are *succ* (or successor) and *pred* (or predecessor) and their functionality is as follows:

succ (ptr):

   ptr := ptr + 1
   IF ptr = buffer size THEN
       ptr := 0

pred (ptr):

   ptr := ptr - 1
   IF ptr < 0 THEN
       ptr := buffer size - 1

The software for the Terminal Manager comprises the following four procedures:

(1) input interrupt procedure
(2) read ch
(3) write ch
(4) output interrupt procedure

input interrupt:

```
{Select the data structures for the interrupting device              }
read char from the input device
IF char = backspace THEN
    {Delete character                                                }
    IF bufinptr <> bufinlin THEN
        {Not at the beginning of the line, so discard previous character}
        pred (bufinptr)
ELSE
IF char = delete line THEN
    bufinptr := bufinlin
ELSE
    {Character to insert, so compute next position in the buffer     }
    succ (bufinptr)
    IF bufinptr = userinlin THEN
        {Buffer full, so discard the character and restore bufinptr  }
        pred (bufinptr)
    ELSE
        inbuffer [bufinptr] := char
        IF char = newline THEN
            bufinlin := bufinptr
            IF job processor is waiting for input THEN
                wake (job processor)
                {This might wake the job scheduler instead           }
                {if the terminal is not logged in                    }
```

read ch:

```
{Select the data structures for this terminal                        }
IF userinptr = bufinlin THEN
    {No input available, so prompt if necessary                      }
    IF bufinptr = bufinlin THEN
        write ch (prompt character)
    suspend
    {Wait until the user has typed a line of input                   }
char := inbuffer [userinptr]
IF char = newline THEN
    userinlin := userinptr
    succ (userinptr)
RETURN (char)
```

write ch (char):

> *{Select the data structures for this terminal* }
> IF useroutptr = bufoutptr THEN
>> suspend
>> *{Wait until the device has emptied the buffer* }
> outbuffer [useroutptr] := char
> succ (useroutptr)
> IF output device idle THEN
>> enable interrupts on the device
>> *{To restart the output interrupt process* }

output interrupt:

> *{Select the data structures for the interrupting device* }
> succ (bufoutptr)
> IF bufoutptr = useroutptr THEN
>> pred (bufoutptr)
>> disable interrupts from the device
>> *{No more characters to output at the moment* }
>> IF job processor is waiting to write ch THEN
>>> free (job processor)
>>> *{The process could be freed as soon as any buffer space is* }
>>> *{available, but it is more efficient, and as convenient,* }
>>> *{to only free when the buffer has been emptied completely* }
> char := outbuffer [bufoutptr]
> write char to the hardware device

Note that for terminal output, the condition of *bufoutptr* being equal to *useroutptr* cannot be used to signify both buffer full and buffer empty condition. Hence *bufoutptr* identifies the last character output and *useroutptr* identifies the next position in the buffer for storing a character. This problem does not arise with the input procedures as a consequence of having the additional line pointers *userinlin* and *bufinlin*.

A3.2 Output System

The Output System provides a printing capability for the system. In this implementation, the interface with user processes occurs indirectly via the file system, where output documents are buffered until printed. The Output System is therefore primarily concerned with retrieving blocks of a document from the File Manager, and for transferring the individual characters to the printer through an interrupt procedure. The user process would 'print' an output document using the *out char* procedure of the File Manager.

A more sophisticated Output System might complement the operation of the Job Scheduler in allowing priority access by ensuring that documents are printed in the most appropriate sequence or priority. It may also take account of special stationery requirements or the peculiar characteristics of different types of printer, if multiple devices are available.

The Output System has been designed as two procedures; one for servicing interrupts from the device and one forming the main body of the Output System process.   This distinction ensures that time-consuming activities such as retrieval of blocks of a file, do not take place within the interrupt procedures, thus helping to maintain responsiveness of the system as a whole.

output system:

    REPEAT
        IF output list empty THEN wait
        select a document from the output list
        open the file for the document
        REPEAT
           read a block of the file
           initialise printptr to the start of the block
           enable interrupts for the device
           {This results in an interrupt from the device, allowing the }
           {interrupt procedure to complete the transfer of the block }
           wait
           {For the block to be output autonomously }
        UNTIL end of document
        close / delete the file
    FOREVER

printer interrupt:

    IF printptr = end of print buffer THEN
        disable interrupts from the device
        free (output system)
        {Wait for another block of characters to print }
    ELSE
        char := printptr ↑
        printptr := printptr + 1
        {Advance pointer to next character (using pointer arithmetic) }

A4 Job Processor

This is the process in which the user program executes. It may be pre-loaded with a range of system utilities to support the user, for example compilers, editors and other useful libraries. It will interface with the rest of the operating system via the interface procedures of the various system modules already outlined.

As the system is capable of supporting a number of user processes that are executing (apparently) at the same time, this module would be replicated for each process in the machine. Although effectively there are multiple copies of this Job Processor module, and each has its own data space, stack and copies of the registers, in practice the code provided within each of the Job Processors is identical and on some machines a single copy of this code can be shared, as described in chapter 5.

job processor:
> *{This implements a simple command interpreter }*
>
> REPEAT
>> read command name from the terminal
>> *{Using the read ch procedure of the terminal manager   }*
>> call the specified utility
>> *{The procedure stop may also be called from here   }*
>> *{to end the execution of the current job   }*
> FOREVER

stop:

> make entry in the output list for documents to be printed
> notify the file manager to close all files
> terminate
> *{Call the job scheduler to deschedule this process   }*

Exercises

1. Produce pseudo-code for a Job Scheduler, which assigns processes (Job Processors) to both interactive users at terminals and background tasks running independently.

   Discuss the impact of allowing background tasks on
       (1) the usability of the system
       (2) system efficiency and throughput.

2. In the design outlined, only one Job Processor at a time is allocated a time slice.

    Extend the design of the simple Process Scheduler to allow multiple Job Processors to be allocated time slices concurrently. Bear in mind the objective of making the Coordinator as simple and efficient as possible.

    What advantages may accrue from this strategy?
    [Hint: see the section on multiprogramming on pages 93-95].

3. Identify what changes would be needed to the Process Scheduler to provide a non-linear scheduling strategy based on process behaviour during a time slice. For example, a suitable strategy might be to allocate longer time slices to processes which are preempted at the end of a time slice, but to make them wait longer between time slices.

    Discuss why this strategy might be desirable.
    [Hint: consider the scheduling and memory management overheads when time-slicing].

4. Discuss why the virtual store interrupt routine might initialise (clear) the page of RAM when it is allocated to a process for the first time.

5. Discuss why the store rejection algorithm would be invoked while there are still free pages of RAM available.
    [Hint: consider the delays to a process when all of RAM is in use].

6. Outline the pseudo-code for the File Manager described in A2.3.

7. What are the performance implications of providing a hierarchical directory structure, particularly when inserting new files within leaf directories?

    How might excessive disk transfers be avoided in providing such a structure?
    [Hint: see chapter 7 and consider whether name aliasing could flatten the hierarchy].

8. When the system restarts, it must discover what free space is available on the disk. Outline strategies based on:

    (1) maintaining a list of free blocks on the disk itself, and
    (2) computing a free list from information held in the file directories.

    Discuss the impact of the different strategies:

    (1) if the system crashes or is shutoff in an uncontrolled way, and
    (2) on the normal restart time of the system.

9. Compare the use of single buffering and cyclic buffering for output to a terminal. Consider both the apparent responsiveness of the system and its overall efficiency.

10. Outline the design of an Output Scheduler if there were multiple printers connected to the computer. How would the design of the Output System change?

11. Discuss the rationale for subdividing the Output System functionality into an interrupt procedure and a separate process. Consider the effect of the system scheduling on the interrupt response time both for the system as a whole and for the output device.

Index